D0471871

Your Self-Motivated
BABY

• • • • •

Also by Beverly Stokes

Amazing Babies Moving: Essential Movement
to Enhance Your Baby's Development in the First Year

Your Self-Motivated
BABY

• • • • •

**Enhance Your Baby's Social and Cognitive Development
in the FIRST SIX MONTHS through Movement**

Beverly Stokes

Foreword by Thomas R. Verny, MD

North Atlantic Books
Berkeley, California

Copyright © 2015 by Beverly Stokes. All rights reserved. No portion of this book, except for brief review, may be reproduced, stored in a retrieval system, or transmitted in any form or by any means—electronic, mechanical, photocopying, recording, or otherwise—without the written permission of the publisher. For information contact North Atlantic Books.

Published by
North Atlantic Books
Berkeley, California

Cover photo © Alena Ozerova/Shutterstock.com
Cover and book design by Jasmine Hromjak
Printed in the United States of America

Back cover photos © iStockphoto.com/DragonImages, © StockLite/Shutterstock.com, © Michel Borges/Shutterstock.com, ©S_L/Shutterstock.com.

MEDICAL DISCLAIMER: The following information is intended for general information purposes only. Individuals should always see their health care provider before administering any suggestions made in this book. Any application of the material set forth in the following pages is at the reader's discretion and is his or her sole responsibility.

Your Self-Motivated Baby: Enhance Your Baby's Social and Cognitive Development in the First Six Months through Movement is sponsored and published by the Society for the Study of Native Arts and Sciences (dba North Atlantic Books), an educational nonprofit based in Berkeley, California, that collaborates with partners to develop cross-cultural perspectives, nurture holistic views of art, science, the humanities, and healing, and seed personal and global transformation by publishing work on the relationship of body, spirit, and nature.

North Atlantic Books' publications are available through most bookstores. For further information, visit our website at www.northatlanticbooks.com or call 800-733-3000.

Library of Congress Cataloguing-in-Publication data
Stokes, Beverly.
  Your self-motivated baby : enhance your baby's social and cognitive development in the first six months through movement / Beverly Stokes ; foreword by Thomas Verny.
     pages cm
  Summary: ""A hands-on parenting guide for working with babies on their physical, social, and cognitive development"—Provided by publisher.
  ISBN 978-1-58394-957-3 (paperback) — ISBN 978-1-58394-958-0 (ebook)
  1. Movement, Psychology of. 2. Cognition in infants. 3. Infants—Development. I. Title.
  BF295.S866 2015

  649'.122—dc23

                        2015021197

1 2 3 4 5 6 7 8 VERSA 19 18 17 16 15

Printed on recycled paper

To all new parents and their babies
as they begin a joyful journey of movement together

● ● ● ● ●

Contents

● ● ● ● ●

Foreword by Thomas Verny   ix

Preface   xi

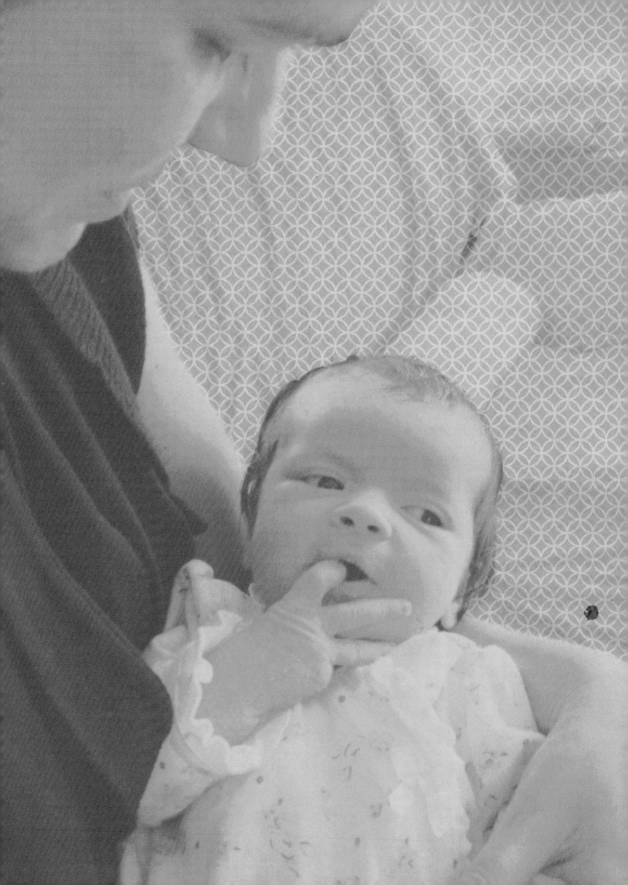

Foreword

● ● ● ● ●

Beverly Stokes's *Your Self-Motivated Baby* is a masterful, clear-eyed, and provocative exploration of a highly neglected subject, namely the amazing abilities of newborns and infants in three areas: social skills, problem solving, and motor movements. Beverly with a glittering and sparkling sensibility shows how babies supported as competent learners become more accomplished at problem solving and move from motivation to mastery. Her innovative approach is based on over twenty-five years of facilitating parent-baby movement sessions as well as a growing body of research that has confirmed that motor-skill acquisition is essential for a baby's neurological development. It seems to me that Beverly has succeeded in discovering a way to connect and communicate with infants by entering their space and exploring it together with them.

By focusing parents' attention on their children's movements, two immensely important things are achieved. Firstly, as indicated above, we support and enhance the growth of the child's neural networks that in the long run will lead to a more intelligent and healthier mind and personality. Secondly, and I suggest more importantly, we contribute to the development of positive bonding and attachment. A caregiver who is reliably available and responsive to a baby's needs forms the basis for secure attachment, for competence in exploring the environment and forming other relationships, and for developing self-esteem. Encouraging attachment gradually gives rise to a system of thoughts, memories, beliefs, expectations, emotions, and behaviors about the self and others. This system continues to develop with time and experience and enables the child to handle new types of social interactions with ease.

The book is furnished with a wealth of beautiful and helpful photographs. Obviously, Beverly is a great observer of babies, which allows her to make surprising and insightful connections. With a keen eye and a caring heart she succeeds in entertaining and informing. This is a disarmingly readable book that presents a panoramic view of the subject. It is essential reading for anyone contemplating having a child, and for all parents with newborns and babies in the first six months.

Thomas R. Verny, MD, DHL, DPsych, FRCPC, FAPA
Editor in chief of the Journal of the Association
for Pre- and Perinatal Psychology and Health (JAPPPAH)

Preface

Every parent wants a healthy, happy, and motivated baby—a baby eager to move, interact, and explore her world. *Your Self-Motivated Baby* provides you with a fresh approach to parenting based on baby movement research and natural movement development. This book is written to provide you with a new way to parent your baby through movement, enjoy your baby more, and enhance your baby's social and cognitive development. Educators and professionals will also find this information invaluable in their work and practice.

In documenting my ongoing parent-baby movement sessions, I was finding, as other infant researchers were, that babies were revealing their competence in their social interactions and goal-directed actions much earlier than previous research had shown. I felt it was essential to document my ongoing parent-baby movement sessions so that parents and caregivers would have this vital information to make a difference for their baby.

In my two-year preparation for this book, I have analyzed and edited thousands of photos, creating compelling vignettes that will inspire, inform, and delight you. New information about infant development is presented in fascinating detail that will enhance your interactions and understanding of what babies can do, how they communicate, and what they know. You will find that each month includes social and play interactions, guided observations, and movement explorations for you to enjoy with your baby.

In interviews with parents, a mother of one of the babies in this book tells us about her experience in following my *Parenting through Movement* program at home with her baby. The following is an excerpt from her six-month review:

Kaya is now into her sixth month and it's amazing to look back at this little baby that I cradled in my arms. My experience of body movement as it relates to my growing and developing child has been truly enriching. I have found a way to connect and communicate with Kaya by entering her space and exploring it together with her. I have found the internal breathing and grounding of my body on the floor a way to find a quiet and calming place for the two of us. And I have found I'm able to discover my own body, all over again.

My passion and profound commitment in writing *Your Self-Motivated Baby* is to inspire you to share in the joy of movement with your baby. I hope it will bring you many hours of pleasure together and will inform and enrich your relationship with your self-motivated baby.

Introduction

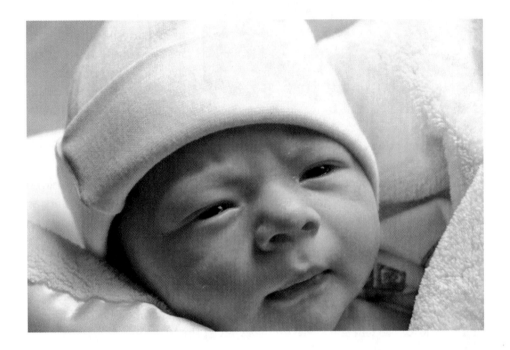

New research findings clearly show that babies develop as self-motivated learners and active participants in social interactions beginning in their first six months. This book provides you—as parent, caregiver, or grandparent—with a new parenting through movement approach that will inspire you and guide you how best to engage and support your baby in his social and cognitive development during this formative time.

Since writing *Amazing Babies Moving*, my book on the baby's essential movement in the first year of life, I have continued my documented research on natural movement development. In this book my movement analyses include important new information about a baby's development in the pre-locomotion period. More specifically, my research on motivation in social and play interactions shows that the baby's early explorations, right from birth, have a much greater influence on their future development than previously thought.

You will learn about the movement framework that I have organized into three main sections: developmental movement, social interaction, and self-motivated learning. These are clearly illustrated in the instructional baby vignettes in color photo sequences. The vignettes are created to show the baby's amazing abilities in all three areas: social skills in leading interactions, problem-solving skills in goal-directed actions, and movement skills in navigating the environment.

My innovative approach is based on over twenty-five years of facilitating parent-baby movement sessions in natural environments. It is essential that parents and caregivers understand the importance of this new documented information for their baby during these early months. Based on this information parents can provide a nurturing environment that encourages their baby's movement, interaction, and exploration.

This book gives you the understanding of the movement foundation for your baby's social and cognitive development that you can build on in the all-important first six months. We will start with an overview of the three main sections.

★ Developmental Movement

During the first half-year babies undergo a dynamic and dramatic change in their development. Using this movement framework will enhance your understanding of how babies move, how they move to communicate, and how they move to learn. Babies progress from lying in a self-contained space—defined by the reach of their arms and legs—to acquiring the ability and skills to move from one place to another, to interact with their parents and caregivers, and to explore their environment.

You will learn how babies develop their body awareness through movement and touch, and organize their body image through a sequence of developmental movement patterns. The book provides parent-baby body awareness games and play activities that support your baby's movement and social development.

Each month contains photo-vignettes demonstrating longer movement sequences initiated by the baby. These vignettes fine-tune your observation skills and deepen your understanding of the essential movements that are primary to your baby's development.

♥ Social Interaction

Movement is also expressive communication. It is now recognized that infants take in more information about others and their environment much earlier than previously thought. You will discover that babies are active participants and can take the lead in their social interactions during these formative first six months.

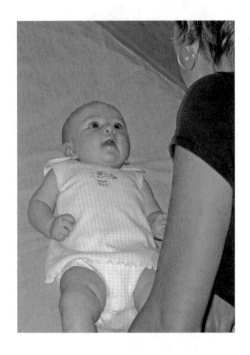

With this book as your guide, you will learn new ways to move and interact with your baby. Parent-baby body games and visual-tracking action songs reinforce your baby's natural movement development. Bonding through movement stimulates parents' spontaneity, and through these age-appropriate play activities parents gain an appreciation of their baby's development. Babies are teaching us so much more than we fully realize.

Parents learn to tune into their baby's expressive communication—the meaning in movement. Engaging in intimate social interactions helps parents recognize their baby's subtle communication cues. Learning new ways to observe and interact through movement builds parenting confidence that enhances bonding with their baby.

● Self-Motivated Learning

Self-motivated learning begins with babies' curiosity and interest in their environment. Integrated developmental movements are essential for the babies' emerging

capabilities in problem solving and goal-directed actions. These self-initiated actions are the foundation for their social and cognitive development.

When you provide your baby with an environment where he can play on his own—trusting in his curiosity and natural ability to problem solve—you support his development. Self-confidence and pleasure in learning are the satisfying results when babies initiate, follow through, and complete their activities at their own pace—from motivation to mastery.

This book will provide you with information for creating an appropriate floor space in your home that encourages your baby's movement, social interactions, and self-motivated explorations.

★ Developmental Movement

The developmental movement sections of *Your Self-Motivated Baby* focus on the baby's movement patterns and learning skills covering the first six months. A dynamic, descriptive framework with text and photo sequences will enhance your observation skills and advance your understanding of the developmental movement process.

Why is it important for parents and caregivers to understand their baby's movement development—especially in these formative first six months? My ongoing research over the past ten years has found that babies reveal their abilities in these three main areas earlier than previously thought. This is corroborated by other major researchers in infant and child development fields.

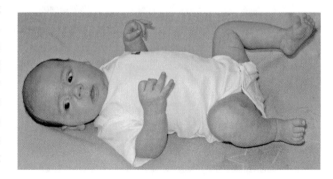

The National Scientific Council on the Developing Child at Harvard University reports that critical features of brain architecture are shaped by experience before and right after birth: different

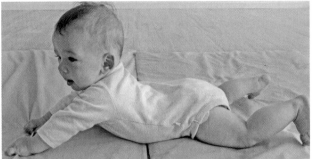

types of experience are essential at different ages for optimal brain development. Starting at birth, basic sensory and social experiences are vital for enhancing the brain's developing neural architecture.[1]

My findings have been further corroborated by the resurgent interest in motor development by infant researchers in the first months of the infant's development. Karen Adolph, a well-known infant researcher at New York University, writes that a growing body of research has confirmed that motor-skill acquisition is essential for a baby's development, serving both as the foundation and catalyst for development; and that early motor-skill achievement impacts all areas of a baby's development—cognitive, perceptive, emotional, and social.[2]

In a ground breaking fourteen-year, large-scale longitudinal research study published in 2013, Marc Bornstein, head of child and family research at the Eunice Kennedy Schriver National Institute of Child Health and Human Development (NICHD), and his associates reported that infants they studied who were more motorically mature and who explored more actively at *five months* achieved higher academic levels when they were fourteen years old. Based on their analysis of the results, they concluded that an infant's greater motor-exploratory competency enables the infant to participate in more opportunities for social interaction and creates richer involvement with their environment. This forms the foundation for the development of better cognitive functioning during childhood and higher academic achievement in adolescence.[3]

Developmental movement focuses on the dynamic foundation for understanding how babies move. There is a general progression to a baby's movement development. As you follow the movement organization through which your baby progresses in the first six months—first lifting her head, rolling, and belly crawling to developing the components for independent sitting—you'll learn to recognize the essential movement patterns that underlie these developmental milestones.

The organization of the photo sequences in the book clearly demonstrates the baby's developmental movement processes. Three key achievements that underlie babies' extraordinary transformation in the pre-locomotion stage are:

- Learning to move and interact with the force of gravity

- Exploring their body awareness and body boundaries

- Developing their body image through a sequence of movement patterns

We start our journey with an overview of selected movement systems, basic movements, and the multimodal systems.

Vestibular System

The vestibular system, which is highly developed at birth, coordinates movement throughout our whole body. The sense of balance is located in the vestibule of the inner ear. The inner ear registers our perception of where we are in relationship to the earth by the pull of gravity. Every movement the baby makes stimulates the vestibular system. From infancy on, we depend on the smooth functioning of this system for visual-movement coordination, locomotion, and balance—all of which contribute to the awareness of where we are in space.

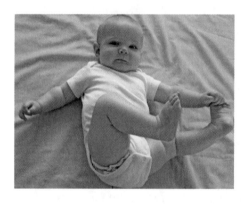

Kinesthetic System

The kinesthetic system provides us with information about our body, in particular the sense of limb position and limb movement. This kinesthetic sense provides babies with an internal body-mapping process that develops an awareness of their body, knowing where each part of their body is, and how it is moving. The close links between body movement, tactile sensations, and visual explorations are fundamental for babies in developing their body awareness. The sense of effort also contributes to the kinesthetic sense through movement force and weight sensations. Without looking at our body, we know where our limbs are.

Proprioceptive System

The proprioceptive system is considered the "body-position" sense that includes balance. Proprioception refers to the sensory input and feedback from the receptors located in the muscles, joints, ligaments, and tendons. In contrast to the kinesthetic system, proprioception has more to do with our body position and awareness of our body in space and its relationship to that space.

Vestibular, Kinesthetic, and Proprioceptive Systems

This six-month-old baby demonstrates all three systems integrated together. Understanding their relationship to gravity, babies can perform amazing balancing actions. Every movement a baby makes stimulates the vestibular system. The kinesthetic sense provides her  with an internal knowing about where each limb is and how it is moving. The proprioceptive system provides her with an awareness of her body in space and relationship to that space.

Basic Movements

Reflexes

Reflexes are automatic responses to external stimuli and establish the baby's basic patterns of function. Goal-directed actions are more complex than reflexes, and are motivated and activated by the baby to interact socially and explore the environment.

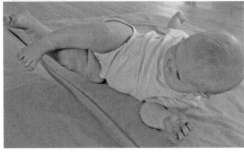

Righting Reactions

Righting reactions enable the baby to raise and maintain her head and body against gravity in all postures, and in transitions from lying down to standing, and to turn in all positions in relationship to gravity and space. Righting reactions begin to develop at birth and remain active throughout life.

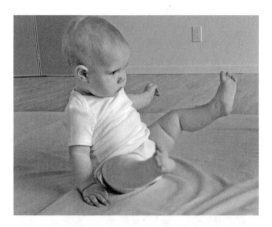

Balance Responses

Balance responses are automatic patterns of response for maintaining balance, which are triggered by shifting of the baby's center of gravity or base of support through space. Most balance responses appear, in concert with the righting reactions, from around six months and then continue throughout life.

Multimodal Senses

As your baby explores and learns about the world, all his senses come into play, providing him with multimodal learning and experiences that include visual, auditory, touch, and kinesthetic stimulation. A baby's early experiences are shaped by these multimodal stimuli and by his developing attention system. He refines his ability to shift focus to pick up information relevant for social inter-

actions and to relate to objects in the environment.

Touch

The skin is the baby's largest sensory organ for touch, and newborns already have a well-developed sense of touch. Babies and parents benefit from bonding through touch and by skin-to-skin contact. Touching and being touched by someone else focuses our attention on our body's sensations.

The sense of touch resulting from active exploration guides our attention to an object's size, shape, weight, texture, and temperature to learn about the external environment.

Haptic System

The haptic system uses sensory information from the cutaneous inputs in
the skin and the kinesthetic input receptors in muscles, tendons, and joints.
It includes tactile and/or kinesthetic
information used for sensing or manipulating objects in the environment. The
kinesthetic system contributes to the
awareness of the position and movement of the baby's arms and legs. Haptic
perception combines with other sensory
modalities such as vision.

Body Awareness

The baby's self-touch sensations and
specific movements—such as hand-to-
mouth, hand-to-hand, hands-to-knees
and hands-to-feet movements—provide
important body awareness organization.
When a baby moves, she experiences
ongoing kinesthetic feedback from her
muscles, joints, and vestibular system.
When the baby watches her arms, legs,
and hands move, she receives consistent
information across visual, touch, and
proprioceptive systems.

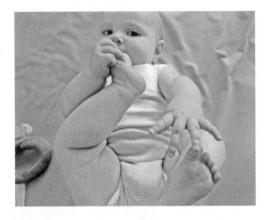

Mouthing

A baby's lips and hands are exquisitely
sensitive, having the largest number
of touch receptors in the body. During
feeding babies learn about the actions

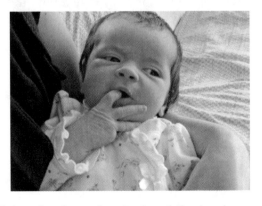

of reaching, grasping, releasing, and withdrawing from the nipple, while simultaneously learning about smell and taste. During the next few months, babies explore
toys and objects by mouthing them. Through mouthing objects babies learn about
specific properties such as hardness, size, shape, and texture.

Vision

Communication in a social interaction involves coordination of gaze, vocalization, movement, and touch with an engaged social partner. Your baby's ability to focus on your face provides a clue to the development of your baby's visual attention and all his visual experiences contribute to his learning. Attention includes focus and explorations such as head turning and visually directed reaching.

Hearing

At birth hearing is well developed and newborns can discriminate their mother's voice. Your baby can identify your voice among all the sounds that make up her rich sonic environment. When you come into a room, even before seeing you, she may smile just hearing the sound of your voice. Tuning into your speech your baby may attend to the rhythm and tempo of your vocal expression—your unique way of communicating. When your baby vocalizes, she experiences the sounds she makes and feedback from shaping her mouth and articulating movements.

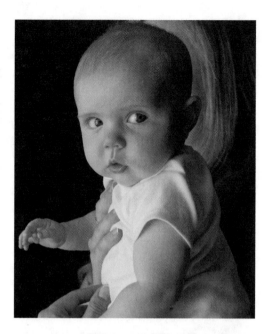

♥ Social Interaction

During the first few weeks of your baby's life, gazing, making facial expressions, vocalizing, listening, and touching are the baby's expressive communication signals. Engaging in these intimate interactions helps parents bond and recognize their baby as a social partner eager to communicate. Thomas Verny, a foremost authority on the effects of the prenatal and early postnatal environment on personality development, writes that the all-important bonding process between infant and parent starts before birth and comes into full fruition in the first weeks and months of the baby's life.[4]

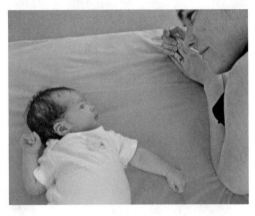

The Social Nervous System

Parents who respond meaningfully to their baby's subtle communication cues expand the baby's social-interaction repertoire. It has been documented that a baby's preverbal social signals stimulate hormones, inducing pleasurable sensations in both the infant and caregiver. Stephen Porges, professor at the University of North Carolina, describes the physiological base for the social nervous system as the protective bonding between parents and their babies, linking the neural regulation of the heart to emotional expression, facial gestures, vocal communication, and social behavior.[5]

The ability to sense his internal bodily processes is essential for an infant's healthy state of well-being. Babies who can self-regulate their physiological states are better able to attend to external cues and take the lead in their social interactions with parents and caregivers.

Visceral System

The visceral system is an internal system that provides a functional awareness of the moment-to-moment changes taking place inside our body. The ability to sense internal states and bodily processes through receptors located on the heart, stomach, liver, and other organs indicate their state of rest and activity. This internal system sends signals that we interpret as feeling hungry, calm, nervous, or joyful.

It is important for parents to recognize these internal body functions, especially upsets of the digestive system, which can cause discomfort in their baby. If the baby is uncomfortable this will lessen his ability to pay attention to the external environment to socialize and organize information in movement-play activities.

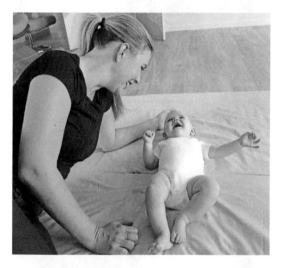

Expressive Communication

Visual Attention

Visual attention conveyed through gazing is an essential preverbal communication signal. When your baby gazes at your face and shifts her gaze between your eyes and your mouth, she expresses her interest and readiness to engage with you.

"Serve and Return" Is a Two-Way Dialogue

The back-and-forth dialogue between a baby and parent has also been described as the "serve and return" in social play as in a fun game of ping pong or tennis. Your baby communicates by looking, gesturing, vocalizing, cooing or crying; and you respond with reassuring looks, comforting words, or by holding your baby close. It's your authentic responses in your everyday interactions with your baby that conveys your wholehearted expression and shapes your baby's expressive communication by keeping the dialogue going.

Gestures Lead Communication

Even in this pre-locomotion stage babies can direct an adult's attention to share their focus of interest. You will learn to fine-tune your observation skills to distinguish your baby's body position, movement, preverbal cues, and signals. Your awareness enhances your social interactions and bonding with your infant.

From the beginning babies are aware that parents and caregivers are interested in what they are doing. Babies build on these social skills and improvise new actions to keep the parent or caregiver engaged.

Interacting with your baby on the floor encourages spontaneity and expands your relationship. What will also be new for you is that you experience the environment from your baby's perspective. As you engage in these play interactions at your baby's level, you, your family, and caregivers will interact with your baby in more expressive dialogues.

● Self-Motivated Learning

Self-motivated learning begins with a baby's curiosity and interest in her environment and with her goal-directed actions leading to new learning experiences. With all their senses actively engaged in experimenting with what their bodies can do, babies develop action plans to do what they 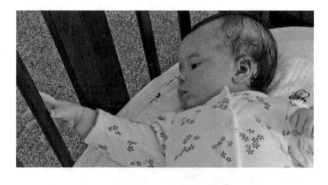 intend to do. These self-motivated actions are guided by the babies' visual attention and pleasure in moving, exploring, and reaching their self-directed goals. When babies are supported as competent learners, they become more accomplished at problem solving and move from motivation to mastery

Bornstein and his research associates at the National Institute of Child Health and Human Development clearly identify the importance of such exploratory behaviors by babies based on their research results. They state the importance of babies developing motor skills and exploration efficiency. These competencies enable babies to gather more information from their environment and differentiate subtle differences in their actions. Becoming more adept in maneuvering and exploring their environment increases the baby's perception and cognitive development for interacting in their expanding complex world.[6]

New Learning Experiences

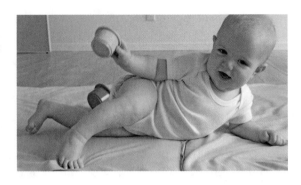

To gain a better understanding of the baby's active explorations in their environment, and specifically their active manual explorations, I turn again to the influence of the haptic and kinesthetic systems.

The haptic features of a toy influence how the baby approaches, grasps, and handles the toy. When babies grasp a toy, the touch receptors in the skin provide information about size, texture, contour, roughness, or smoothness of the object. This information is tactile or, to use a more precise term, haptic. When babies use more force to grasp and hold onto the object, the information they receive about the movement and position of their hand relative to the object is kinesthetic.

Each developmental movement pattern expands the baby's interactions in the environment, which in turn propels the baby's learning to new levels. The baby's postural control in all four body positions—lying on the back, on the front, and on each side—provides babies with new opportunities for exploring and handling toys. In each of these positions, babies experience the size, shape, and weight of a toy or object differently. By grasping, handling, and fingering toys or objects, babies learn to distinguish these different physical properties.

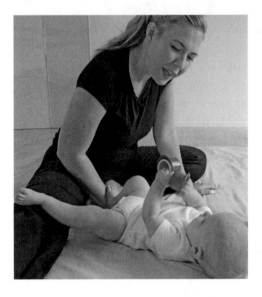

Executive Functioning in Babies

The Center on the Developing Child at Harvard University emphasizes the vital importance of a range of early experiences on the development of effective capacities that underlie the intentional, goal-directed behaviors required for success in daily life. The researchers clearly state that we are not born with the skills to control our impulses, make plans, and stay focused on our goals, but only with the potential to develop these essential capacities. Whether an infant develops them or not depends on his experiences starting from birth and continuing throughout childhood and adolescence.[7]

Understanding the developmental movement process is essential for refining observation skills to better understand what babies are doing and how they perform their actions so that parents and caregivers can support their infant's development.

As a developmental movement specialist with a particular interest in the baby's development and as a movement pattern analyst focusing on the decision-making process in individuals, I have extensively studied the roots of decision-making processes by looking at how babies acquire the ability to plan and act in a goal-directed way.

Following are three stages of the decision-making process based on the movement pattern analysis framework pioneered by Warren Lamb that I have adapted here to use with babies in the first six months; he emphasizes that this framework is distinctive because it relates directly to movement, which can be observed. In his observation of babies and children he recognized that the order of the decision-making process follows the developmental sequence of how children learn to move and play.[8]

Three Stages of Decision Making in Babies

Attention

Curiosity motivates the baby to move and play. Babies are dynamic explorers, and reaching for a desired toy can present new movement challenges. Play is a functional activity which provides the dynamic experiences that encourage problem-solving skills.

Intention

Intention forms the link between the baby's preliminary attention and her decision to act. Babies pay attention to the available information in the environment to create effective action plans so they can move their body into new positions.

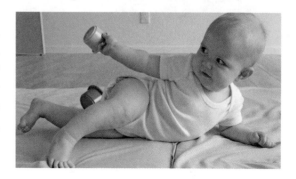

Action

Babies learn to anticipate weight-shifting and can make postural adjustments prior to reaching. Reaching, grasping, and handling objects require new timing strategies to successfully accomplish their goal-directed actions.

This movement framework sheds light on the decision-making process in babies by providing a new understanding of the baby's developmental abilities in focusing, planning, and problem solving. Motor control is an essential part of executive functioning. What I am finding is that babies are able to integrate a complex sequence of movement patterns; they can maintain postural control to explore toys and objects and are able to choreograph multi-step processes expanding their movement-repertoire problem solving in play.

Now with this book as your guide, you are ready to begin the exciting journey of learning about your baby's development in these formative first six months.

Month One

• • • • •

Beginning the Developmental Dance

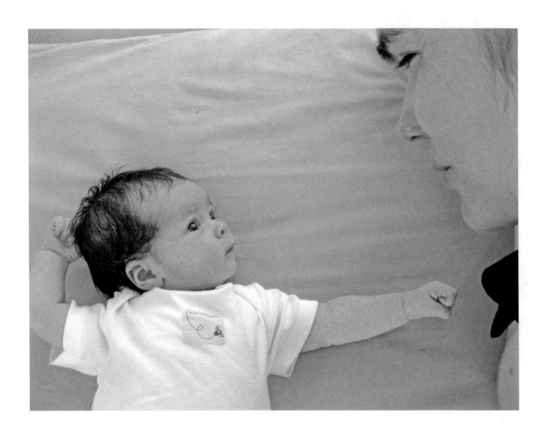

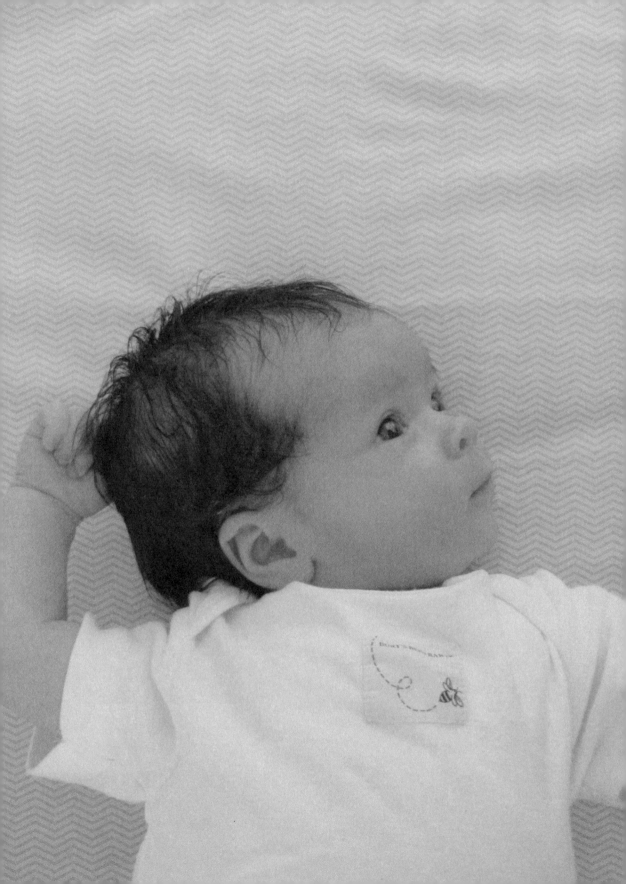

Sleeping and resting in these early months is necessary for your new baby's physical health and well-being. Your baby's relationship to gravity is primary to his security, comfort, growth, and development. It is essential that babies bond to the earth's pull so they can rest, allowing their bodies to yield to the force of gravity.

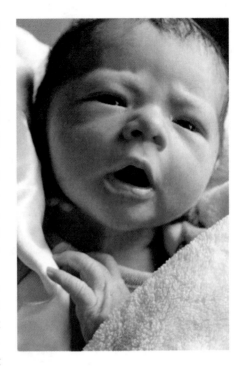

When your baby is awake and alert, he is *moving.* Your baby's movement is fundamental for his social and cognitive development. Movement is the connection that integrates your baby's dynamic expressive communication and his motivation to explore.

Attuning to your baby and reading his preverbal cues and signals lets him know you understand what he is interested in and what he's communicating. Responding appropriately to your baby's signals is an important skill that will enhance your growing relationship and increase your pleasure in parenting.

Each baby is unique and develops in tune with his own rhythm and timing. By being attentive to your baby's movement and communication cues, you are developing a deep appreciation for his remarkable abilities and unfolding accomplishments.

★ Developmental Movement

Exploring Gravity

In the womb, your baby's spine was flexed in a c-curve shape. Now at one month, as your baby uncurls her arms and legs, she is already more extended than when she was a newborn. Your baby's learning begins with gravity and her body. Developing in close relationship to the earth's pull, your baby's movements progress from yielding to gravity to pushing away from the force of gravity.

When your baby lies on the front of her body, in the prone position, lifting her head and pushing down with her forearms or hands she is exploring gravity and its pull on her body. Babies develop strength by pushing their whole body weight against the resistance of gravity. Each antigravity movement clarifies the baby's connection

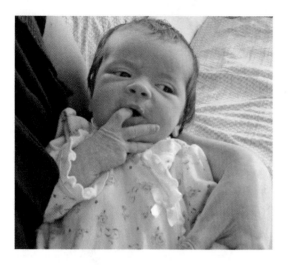

to this force. When babies learn to interact with gravity first by yielding and then by pushing, they develop a comfortable relationship or balance with the earth's force as a foundation for future movement explorations.

Body Awareness

Each month you will learn how babies embody themselves through their own physical movements, touch, and body-on-body contact. The close link between your baby's body movements, specific tactile sensations, and visual processing informs him about himself from the beginning. We see this two-week-old baby's early developing body awareness in the way she mouths her index finger and touches her cheek and chin with her other fingers.

With these self-initiated movement explorations your baby develops an awareness of her body and her body's boundaries, knowing where each part of her body is and how it is moving.

Spinal-Movement Patterns: Front and Back of Our Body

Spinal movements differentiate the front of our body from the back and develop an integrated spinal axis. These movements provide the internal core support for your baby to begin coordinating her arms and legs in relationship to each other and in relationship to her whole body.

One-month-old babies can turn their head farther to one side. With improved lateral vision, babies begin tracking from the side to midline. With the pull of gravity, the baby's arms are moving away from her body.

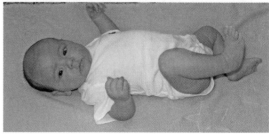

Spinal-movement patterns establish the baby's head-to-tail connection in all four body positions—lying on her front, back, and each side.

The Navel-Star Pattern

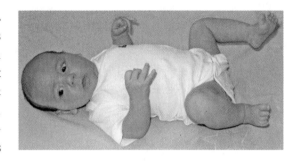

The navel-star pattern establishes internal body connections between the navel and all six "limbs" that coordinate into the more specific developmental-movement patterns. This is a total-body flexion or total-body extension pattern that begins at the navel and radiates through the body to all six limbs—head, tailbone, arms, and legs.

When babies extend all their limbs or flex all their limbs in a simultaneous movement, you can observe that the impulse begins at the navel. Because it typically takes several months for babies to develop good head and neck control, it is important to support your baby's head, neck, and spine in all positions.

♥ Social Interaction

Embracing and Holding Your Baby

Babies thrive on their parents' loving touch. Holding and cuddling is essential for every baby's sense of body comfort and healthy development. As you embrace your baby in your arms—in a face-to-face, body-to-body position—he gets to know your facial expressions, your voice, and the way you move.

In the Horizontal Position

When you cradle your baby in the horizontal position, you support his spine in a c-curve shape that prompts your baby to curl his arms and legs around his navel center and cuddle into you. Babies receive different sensory input depending on which side of your body you hold them on. With their mouths, babies learn about the actions of reaching, grasping, releasing, and withdrawing from the nipple in breast or bottle feeding.

In the Vertical Position

Parents typically hold their babies in a vertical position after feeding or when standing and walking to calm them. When you place your baby in this upright position, you can rest her head on your body with her head turned to one side. You will want to support her head in line with her body to maintain her spinal alignment from head to tail.

In the vertical position, your baby will soon learn to hold her head in line with her body without letting her head fall forward, backward, or to one side.

Expressive Communication

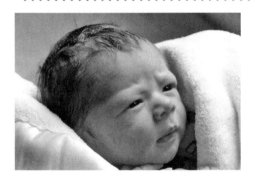

Research shows that babies have many visual abilities and that their visual experience is already well-organized in the first month. Even at birth a baby's visual acuity is good enough so that while lying in your arms, he can see many features of your face: your eyes, your mouth, your nose, and your smile.

A newborn can actively focus and follow your animated expressions: your eyes and eyebrows raised in wonder; your mouth and lips changing shape, widening when you are smiling, and forming a variety of shapes when you are singing, vocalizing vowels, and talking. All these expressive early experiences show your baby's recognition of his parents and caregivers.

Gazing Face-to-Face

Shaping your arms in a c-curve and holding your baby in the familiar horizontal position supports your intimate relationship and social interactions. In this position your baby is attracted to your facial expressions and may respond to you by gazing and making little sounds.

Authentic "You-ness"

When you cradle your baby in your arms, your baby quickly senses how you are feeling. In your body-to-body interactions your baby picks up a variety of cues from you including your breathing rhythm, arm pressure, vocal tone, and expressive body actions. Your baby can quickly tell if you're relaxed and happy, rushed, or upset. She doesn't have to put all your separate actions together, for it is the sense of authentic "you-ness" flowing through your actions and interactions that your baby responds to.

Expressive Communication Beginnings

Recent research shows that one of the most essential experiences in shaping the architecture of the developing brain is the "serve and return" interaction between infants and their parents or caregivers. In this developmental game, the baby may initiate a social interaction instinctively through babbling, facial expressions, and gestures; and the parent responds in a directed, meaningful way.

Back-and-Forth Communication

Engaging in this face-to-face social interaction a parent and baby learn to follow each other's facial expressions and tongue movements. When you hold and position your baby in front of you, notice your baby's attention and focus on your changing expressions.

It has been well documented that newborns can mimic a parent's tongue protrusion game.

Research also finds that newborns, after a little time, started to initiate the previously imitated gestures.

Observe your baby and let him take the lead in your next expressive social interaction.

Your Expressive Baby—Face-to-Face

The following social interaction, which takes place in a natural setting, will provide you with examples of ways to engage your baby's attention.

Gazing at her mother's face

Babies use their eyes for information. This baby's attention is engaged, gazing at her mother's face. Looking closer, we notice in this face-to-face interaction, Isabelle's gaze is focused on her mother's eyes, her right arm is active, and her right hand is softly open.

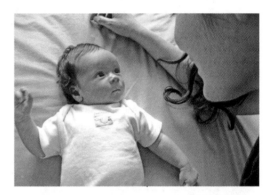

Gaze shift

Isabelle's mother is talking and vocalizing a variety of vowel sounds that attracts her baby's attention. Isabelle shifts her gaze from her mother's eyes to her mother's animated facial expressions.

Babies are responsive to vowel sounds in a back-and-forth interaction.

Engaged in this dialogue with her mother, Isabelle expressively participates by raising and extending her arm.

Her mother keeps the dialogue going.

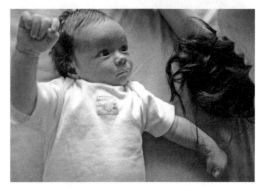

Vowels and Body Actions

Based on his research, Stephen Porges writes that positive forms of communication, which include vocalizations, are important components of successful care giving, and, as is shown here, of parenting as well. There are also additional benefits from the interactive effect between social communication and internal visceral systems, namely, more positive social experience and increased health.[1]

Vocalizing vowels

The energy of the vowel sounds provides infants with a means by which they can explore their own actions.

As her mother says the vowels in a sing-song voice, Isabelle focuses on her mother's changing facial expressions. Her mother's mouth expands, and Isabelle looks at the middle of her face, at her nose, and at her cheeks which change shape as her mother smiles and vocalizes.

Ah vowel

The position of her mother's open mouth lengthens into a new oval shape. Shifting her gaze to focus on her mother's mouth, Isabelle may also notice the changing position of her mother's tongue as she actively responds to her mother's vocalized *"ah"* vowel sound.

Oh vowel

Isabelle looks up at her mother's eyes and eagerly responds through her whole body. She expressively interacts, shaping her mouth in an o-shape that mimics the shape of her mother's vocalizing mouth.

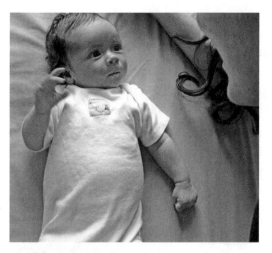

Rhythmic Dialogue

Colwyn Trevarthen, Emeritus Professor of child psychology at the University of Edinburgh, has shown through his research that newborns can take the initiative to build relationships with caregivers through smiling and eye contact in intimate dialogues.[2]

The active elements in the baby's expressive communication cues are visual processing, vocalizing, gestures, and touch contact. As you observe this baby's hand movements, notice her gestures are more expressive and articulate as she actively participates in a preverbal dialogue with her mother.

Shaping Her Hand Gestures

In rhythmic resonance with her mother, Isabelle opens her thumb, index, and middle finger in a circular shape that mirrors the shape of her mother's mouth in vocalizing.

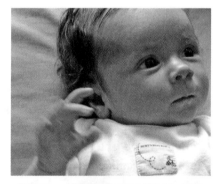

Looking and listening with rapt attention, she is anticipating "what comes next." Ready to participate, notice how her articulate, rhythmical hand movements are conducting her communication. She closes her hand tightly enclosing her index finger under her thumb.

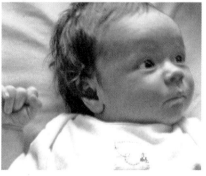

Her shift in focus, varying touch pressure in her hands, and spontaneous timing give us glimmers of the expressive gestures that will accompany her preverbal expression and talking rhythms. She extends her arm and moves her index finger on top of her thumb.

Shifting her gaze to her mother's open mouth stimulates Isabelle to open her hand and extend all her fingers and thumb. We can see the shape that her thumb, index, and middle finger make.

Gazing at her mother's open mouth she brings her thumb and middle finger together, raising her index finger higher. Could it be that Isabelle notices her mother's tongue that is in a higher position in her mouth?

Shifting her gaze again, she looks directly at her mother's eyes. Isabelle responds with her whole body, direct focus, and open mouth. She gestures with a softly flexed hand. Her thumb contacts the side of her middle finger and tip of her index finger, but her fourth and fifth fingers aren't touching the palm of her hand.

From the beginning your baby's gestures have social meaning; gazing and gestures are the baby's expressive communication cues. Infant research finds that in order for a baby to imitate an adult's facial expressions in a social interaction, the baby needs to attend to the facial expressions of the adult to produce her own matching expressions, and integrate her proprioceptive feedback with the facial expressions of the adult.

Isabelle's open-hand gestures reflect the changing shapes of her mother's mouth vocalizing the vowels. A baby's hand gestures may also synchronize with the rhythms of the parent's playful speech.

The nimble movement between this baby's thumb, index finger, and middle finger is a significant social gesture. It reveals Isabelle's fine-motor dexterity and intention to interact, articulating her expressive social participation and relationship with her mother.

At this early stage, these movements demonstrate the baby's active focus, and her rhythmical responses communicate her active participation in this longer social sequence. The baby's responsiveness and pleasure in these early expressive dialogues enhance the growing parent-baby relationship while at the same time building parenting confidence.

Attunement to Your Preverbal Baby

Learning to attune to your preverbal baby's expressive communication cues, movements, and actions requires practice. In the beginning your interactions take place with your baby cradled in your arms and supported on your lap. When your baby begins moving and playing on the floor with you by her side, you can respond appropriately to her communication cues, and your social interactions begin to expand.

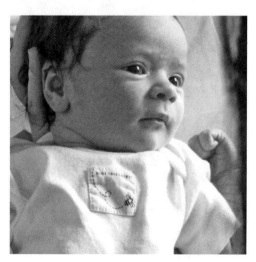

Attention

In these early months, you will be observing your baby's:

- Alertness and sleep times
- Breathing and digesting rhythms
- Comfort and discomfort

As you recognize and respond to your baby's needs, you see how these everyday experiences help you develop and fine-tune your observation skills.

Attunement

Notice when your baby is alert and attentively gazing at you. Your baby communicates how she feels through her subtle expressive-communication cues: gazing, smiling, moving, touching, vocalizing, and gesturing.

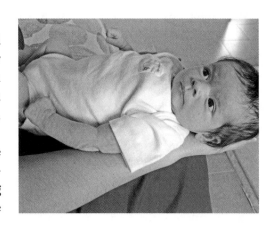

With experience you will become more finely attuned to your baby's signals and respond appropriately, letting your baby know you understand the meaning in her communication.

Breathing Rhythms and Humming

Holding and aligning your body in relationship to your baby encourages you and your baby to engage and interact in different body positions. Your baby's expressions reflect her internal processes: her comfort and discomfort in breathing and digesting. During your humming explorations, you will become aware of your breathing rhythm. When you exhale, notice that your breathing deepens and a reflexive inhalation spontaneously occurs.

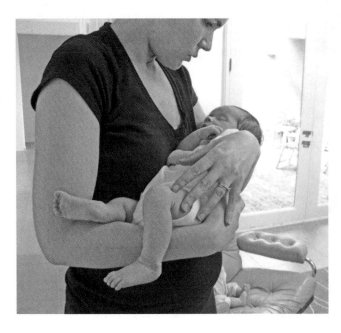

Humming sounds

Become aware of the sensation in your lips.

On an exhalation begin making humming sounds and notice a subtle vibrating sensation between your lips: *"hmmm hmm-mm."* These sound vibrations from your body soothe your baby. Parents often add little sounds with their facial expressions.

When you are humming and your baby looks at you, smile and let the tone of your voice rise. Notice your baby's response. Next time, when the tone of your voice rises, you may notice you expressively raise your eyebrows.

As you notice your breathing rhythms, you'll experience an increased vitality, and your new sense of well being will have a calming effect on your baby. All forms of vocalized sounds—humming, singing, crying, and speaking—promote breathing by exercising the respiratory system.

Walking Rhythms Calm Your Baby

Parents know that crying babies usually calm down when they are picked up and carried, but they may not understand why carrying the baby has such a calming effect. Recent research has confirmed that the calming response is dependent on the tactile inputs and proprioception from the motion in the parent's walking rhythm.

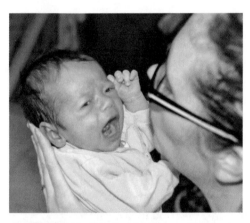

Your baby's digestive system

As your baby experiences moment-to-moment visceral changes, he lets you know how he is feeling: crying if he is hungry, squirming if he has indigestion, or cooing when he is satisfied.

Walking and talking rhythms

Holding your baby while walking, add sounds—talking, or singing to your baby. Begin by increasing and decreasing your vocalizing rhythms to match the intensity of your baby's crying sounds—*"Oh,"* *"Oh oh,"* *"Ohhh."* When your baby calms down and feels comfortable, you can add new humming sounds.

Walk slowly, swing, and sway

You can calm and soothe your baby by walking slowly, stopping to sway side-to-side, while making soft sounds or singing lullabies. Over the first few months you may respond to your baby's vocalizing with *"ah,"* and add more drawn-out vowel combinations like *"ahh-ohh-ooo."*

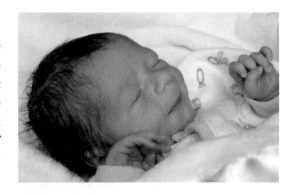

● Self-Motivated Learning

When babies are supported in their development as self-directed learners, they create their own action plans and problem-solving activities, progressing from motivation to mastery. The foundation starts this month with your baby's development of attention, focus, and shifting focus—all of which help babies organize their senses to pick up relevant information in social interactions and actions in their environment.

Curiosity and interest is what motivates babies to explore and initiate goal-directed actions. Self-confidence develops when babies complete their explorations in their own time, moving from motivation to mastery.

Purposeful Play

Babies are not just reflexive but are purposeful in their movement and play. Even newborns can turn their head and eyes in the direction of a voice or sound. Turning toward a sound also provides visual information about who or what is making the sound. Babies begin to match what they see with what they hear in multimodal sensory integration.

Freedom to Move and Play

Space on the Floor for Two

Create a floor space for your everyday movement play with your baby.

Choose a natural cotton play mat or exercise mat—large enough for two—that fits your space on your floor. If you choose fabric that is soft and textured it will provide tactile stimulation to your baby's skin.

The best play time for your baby is when your baby is rested, fed, dry, calm, and alert.

The best time for you is when you can calmly focus on what your baby is doing for an uninterrupted period of time.

This is your baby's first movement play space. Here your curious baby can move his body and explore in a safe nurturing environment. When you are on the floor next to him, your baby feels secure and content at his appropriate developmental level. Each month I will provide new information for you to refine and expand your observation skills in all the new movements and actions your baby is doing.

Uninterrupted Play

Uninterrupted play is best when babies are alert and content moving their body and exploring their environment. Observe, listen, and learn as each new exploration captures your baby's attention. Pause and wait until your baby sends you a little signal and follow your baby's lead. Enjoy watching your baby during this quiet time, and every day jot down a few things you notice about your baby's movement and expressive communication.

Unstructured Play

Unstructured play is initiated by the baby and not structured by the parent or caregiver. Often these little explorations in the first few months go unnoticed. But as you will learn, when your baby is quietly playing on his own in his crib or bassinette he is exploring and problem solving, making his own discoveries.

One Month Chapter Review

● ● ● ● ●

DEVELOPMENTAL MOVEMENT

- Relationship to gravity: Gravity is primary to your baby's security, comfort, growth, and development.
- Body awareness: Touch provides babies with essential information in their mouthing hands and fingers explorations.
- Spinal-movement patterns: The spinal patterns develop head-to-tail: extension, flexion, lateral flexion, and rotation.
- Spinal-movement patterns: These patterns differentiate the front of the body from the back and develop an integrated spinal axis.
- Navel-star patterns: These patterns establish internal body connections between the navel and all six limbs.
- Mouthing: Babies learn about the actions of reaching, grasping, releasing, and withdrawing from the nipple in feeding.

SOCIAL INTERACTION

- Bonding: Babies recognize and discriminate their mother's face and voice.
- Engagement: Parent and baby gaze in close mutual awareness of each other.
- Face-to-face: Baby gazes at parent's face and responds to facial expressions.
- Tongue movement: Baby mimics adult tongue movements.
- Attunement to preverbal cues: These cues let your baby know you understand and are interested in the message.
- "Serve and return": Babies may initiate this developmental game and parents respond meaningfully.

One Month Chapter Review (cont.)

● ● ● ● ●

SELF-MOTIVATED LEARNING

- Purposeful play: Babies are not just reflexive, but are purposeful in their movement play.
- Head turning: Newborns turn their head and eyes in the direction of a sound.
- Visual information: Babies match what they see with the sound they hear.
- Vocalizes: A baby experiences her vocal mouth movements and hears the sounds she makes.

Month Two

• • • • •

Making Connections through Movement

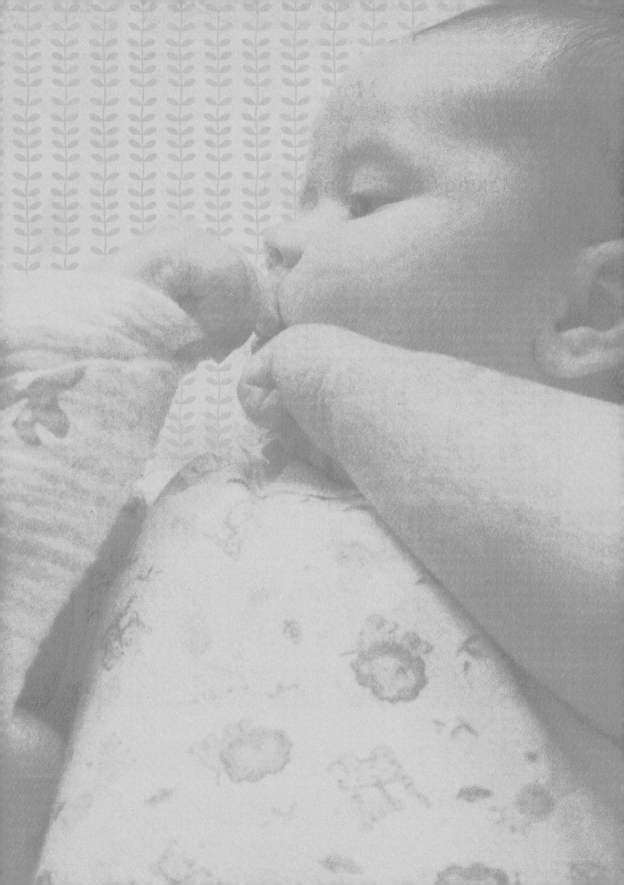

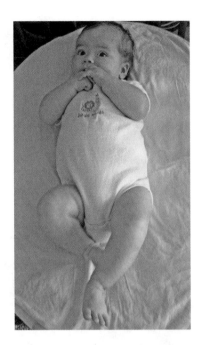

Two-month-old babies are more alert and can link up all forms of sensory information through their body movement. Even before birth your baby's hearing was well developed. Now, at two months lying on her tummy with her head turned to one side, she can orient to a sound behind her.

Your baby is interested in everyone around her. Her smiles are beaming right at you and she is able to take the lead in social interactions too. Smiling, vocalizing, and turning toward and away from stimulation are the preverbal cues that communicate what your baby is interested in. When family and caregivers respond to the meaning in these preverbal cues, she knows they understand her.

Babies wave, circle, and cycle their arms and exercise a variety of kicking patterns to enhance their motor development. Through these patterns of flexion and extension, babies can sense how each part of their body is moving. Your baby's fine sense of touch and tactile body explorations contribute to his developing body awareness.

Two-month-old babies can coordinate their arm actions to make more connections between the things they see, feel, and touch. Eye-hand coordination and tactile investigations inform them about the special properties of objects in their environment. Two-month-old babies are already problem solving to reach their goals.

★ Developmental Movement

Movement Coordination

During this month your baby is gaining control of his arms and legs. He can bring his arms across his chest, holding and mouthing his hands. Babies exercise a variety of kicking patterns that enhance their motor development. Through two-phase patterns of flexion and extension, a baby can sense how each part of his body moves, as well as the relationship between his arms and legs.

Kinesthetic Awareness

Your baby's ability to sense the movement of his arms and legs contributes to his growing kinesthetic awareness; his movements inform him where each limb is in space, how each limb is moving, and the quality of rest between these actions.

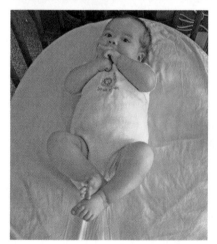

Activity and Rest

As hip flexion decreases, hip extension increases. In between cycles of kicking activity, two-month-old babies can rest their legs with the lateral borders of their feet touching the mat.

Resting may not mean stopping all her body movements. In this example she alternates resting her legs with bringing both hands together and mouthing her hands.

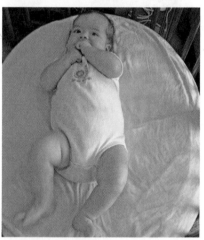

Body-on-Body Explorations

Bringing the feet together provides vital sensory input through a variety of tactile foot-on-foot explorations. These articulated foot movements and body-on-body explorations provide important tactile information for coordinated actions between hands and feet.

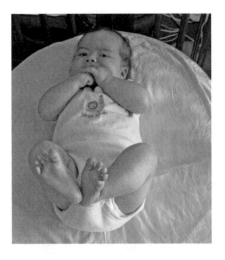

Body Awareness

The interconnections the baby is making between her hands, mouth, and feet develop her body awareness, preparing her for more dynamic play explorations with objects in the environment.

Kicking their legs strengthens the babies' leg muscles in preparation for the locomotion stage: belly crawling, hands-and-knees creeping, climbing, and walking. In the months to come when you see your toddler running, jumping, and hopping, you can look back and see how the simple flexion and extension movements of your two-month-old baby have become integrated into these later locomotion patterns.

Self-Directed Actions

Isabelle is rested, fed, dry, and alert. Lying in her bassinet on her back, in the supine position, she can briefly maintain her head and focus in midline.

Two-month-old babies are more alert and aware of their environment. With more control of her actions Isabelle is exploring her bassinet.

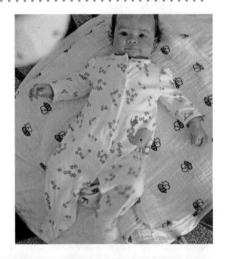

Reaching

She turns her head to the right side and reaches with her right hand to touch the spindle of her bassinet.

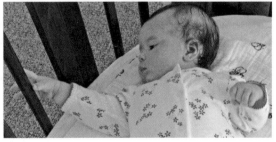

Grasping

She repeats this movement, positioning her right hand to grasp the spindle. Her fingers are on one side and her thumb is on the other side of the spindle. Her left hand remains flexed during this action.

Attention

Isabelle extends her right arm upward in space and focuses on her hand. Regulating her visual attention facilitates her voluntary reaching movements.

Notice her right index finger is curled over her thumb. Her left arm, fingers, and thumb touch her body, and at the same time she isolates her left index finger, mimicking the shape of her right index finger.

Isabelle repeats the action and reaches and touches the spindle again before changing her body position.

When Isabelle coordinates her arm actions, she makes more connections between what she feels, touches, and sees within her arm's reach and visual field. She can regulate her attention and with control reach and touch the oval spindle.

Isabelle repeats the action by sliding her hand through the space and, at the same time, adjusting her hand position to grasp the spindle between her thumb and fingers. Her ability to direct her arm and hand to successfully grasp the spindle demonstrates her problem-solving skills. Eye-hand coordination, the kinesthetic sense, and tactile information about size, hardness, shapes, and space come into play.

All of these functions enhance her cognitive development. In addition, self-produced actions and successful movement explorations build body confidence and contribute to the baby's ability to reach her future goals.

Articulating New Actions

Grasping

Lying in the supine position on the floor on top of her goldfish blanket, Isabelle grasps the edge of her blanket with her right hand and holds onto it with her fingers and thumb.

She gazes at her index finger that is flexed on top of her thumb, and her thumb is under her other fingers.

Mouthing and Touch

A baby's lips and fingers are highly sensitive and contain the highest concentration of touch-receptor cells in the body. Isabelle brings her right hand to her mouth and discriminates specific sensations by mouthing her fingers.

She skillfully moves her thumb on top of her fingers and her index finger contacts her thumb.

The baby's fine sense of touch in her tactile body explorations provides her with essential information that contributes to her developing body awareness.

Extending Her Index Finger

Grasping and holding onto her blanket with her fingers, she pulls on the blanket with one hand and reaches upward, extending both arms. Holding onto her lightweight blanket provides a new textural experience to her hands and arms. She matches what she sees with the tactile information she experiences through the sensory receptors located in the skin, especially to her hands and fingers. This tactile sensory information enables her to match what she sees with what she experiences by grasping, holding, and reaching.

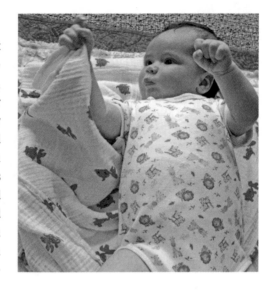

The ability to extend her arm and look at her hand is significant in the development of her eye-hand coordination. She actively focuses on her right hand, beginning to extend her index finger.

We look close-up at her articulate hand movements while holding onto her light blanket. By changing the position of her thumb and placing her thumb on top of her fingers, Isabelle is able to isolate and extend her index finger.

Before a baby can use her index finger in a pointing gesture, she needs to produce the action. We will review this action in a social context in Month Four.

♥ Social Interaction

Kinesphere: The Natural Boundary of Personal Space

Babies extend their arms and legs, reaching with their hands and feet to define the natural boundary of personal space around their body. In adults, the kinesphere is defined as the personal reach space around the body, without taking a step.

Two-month-old babies lying in the supine or prone position are quite content to develop their body awareness in their natural personal space—the space defined by the reach of their arms and legs.

When you are on the floor at your baby's level, you encourage her spontaneous touch responses. With each change of your body position, your baby discovers new ways to interact with you.

Babies often stay in contact with their parents and caregivers by touching them with hands or feet. Connecting through their feet provides abundant tactile sensation. Babies can vary the intensity of foot contact from a light to firm pressure with one or both feet. Stay close enough to your baby so she can make contact with you within her near-reach space, frequently touching you within the area of her kinesphere, sometimes referred to as the bubble of space around our body.

Two Kinespheres

Consider the parent or caregiver sitting on a sofa or chair, watching or talking to her baby from that position. The adult acts within her personal kinesphere from a place that the baby can't see, let alone reach. Although the parent can see the baby within her visual field, the baby's visual attention and movement is limited to his personal kinesphere on the floor.

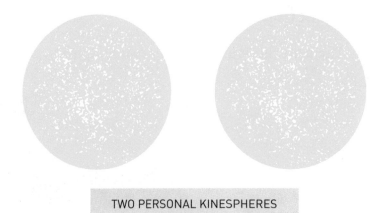

TWO PERSONAL KINESPHERES

TWO KINESPHERES SHARING IN A SPHERE OF ENGAGEMENT

Now consider the relationship between two kinespheres when the parent interacts with her baby on the floor. When two kinespheres overlap I call this the "sphere of engagement."

On the floor, a parent can relate to her two-month-old baby in different orientations and with variable spaces between them.

Face-to-Face Communication

Your face-to-face interactions with your baby are really whole-body experiences. When babies and parents gaze and smile at each other, they respond with their whole body.

Parents often begin their face-to-face communication with exaggerated facial expressions. In these interactions, parents can start by taking cues from their baby and improvise by adding new expressions. Here are some possibilities:

- Open your eyes and mouth wide to communicate surprise.
- Smile to show you are enjoying this interaction.
- Vocalize and talk to your baby about what you are doing.

Your changing facial expressions capture your baby's interest and by adding different sounds and talking to her, you keep the game going. These playful interactions facilitate your baby's ability to integrate her multisensory sensations into a unified experience.

Vocalizing Vowels

Attuned to your voice your baby will respond to your sounds—to your vocalizing and singing, and your expressive rhythm and melodic voice.

Looking at your baby, notice the little shapes she makes with her mouth. You can shape your mouth and expressively respond to your baby's vowel sounds —cooing like the vowel sounds you are making during an exhalation.

Over the first few months, you can continue to respond to your baby's vocalizing *"ah, ah"* and add more drawn-out vowel sounds—*"ahh-ohh-ooo"*—and consonant combinations that grow in intensity such as *"woo-woo-woo."*

Touch

Haptic communication, often known as haptics, is nonverbal communication focused on touch. Touch enhances our social interactions, reinforcing our connection with others that begins at birth. Our skin is the largest sense organ of our body filled with many sensory nerves and the sense of touch is spread over the entire body that informs us about ourselves, about others, and our environment. Babies receive ongoing touch and body-to-body contact in their daily interactions with their parents and caregivers, contributing to the development of the baby's healthy nervous system.

Social Smiling

Social smiling is one of the most delightful interactive features of a budding two-month-old baby. Parents are thrilled when they notice their baby's first smiles. When your baby sees your animated face, she responds head-to-toe with a beaming face and body wriggle.

Babies enjoy smiling and eliciting smiles from others. As a baby leads the interaction with her beaming smile, she looks with interest at her mother's mouth to see her joyful, smiling response. Spontaneity in everyday care-giving interactions provides a variety of ways to interact.

Vocalizing and Expressive Movement

As you become more experienced at interpreting and understanding your baby's expressive sounds, you also notice your baby's responses to your body movements and sounds. You can add head and upper body movements. You can modulate the sound of your voice when moving in closer to your baby, and then moving away. Your baby will follow the flow of your actions and sounds closely, and these responsive social interactions contribute to your back-and-forth vocalizing sequences.

Experiment by noticing how your baby responds when you raise or lower your voice and when you move your head and upper body closer, and then move away. These variations allow you to extend your playtime for as long as your baby is actively engaged.

In social interactions babies regulate their excitement by turning away from the source of stimulation. This helps your baby calm down. Babies also suck their thumb, fingers, or hands; and they make little humming sounds to soothe themselves. When you are attuned to your baby's communication cues, you will know—before your baby becomes over stimulated—that it's time to tone down the exciting activities.

Parent Whole Body Exploration

Nonverbal Communication

With the multiple demands parents need to take care of each day, gaining an awareness of releasing their own bodies' tension is essential. Before engaging with their baby, it is important for parents to tune into their breathing so that they can pause and slow down. For this exploration, first find a moment and place to sit comfortably.

- Begin saying, *"la,la,la,la,la"* and on your next breath, whisper, *"la,la,la,la,la."* Notice how your breathing flows when you are exhaling and then become aware of your reflexive inhalation. Continue for a few breathing cycles and, as your breathing deepens, become aware of your body's tension releasing.

- Now close your eyes. Let yourself begin to smile. Your breathing becomes fuller and you will feel more calm and centered.

This sense of harmony in your postures, gestures, and tone of voice conveys your authentic you-ness to your baby.

Visual Tracking

Your baby's eyes are beginning to converge, focus, and work together. You can observe his developing visual coordination in this activity. Place your baby in the supine position (lying on his back) on the floor.

In your right hand, hold a toy or object about ten to twelve inches away, in line with his visual focus. Move the toy or object horizontally beginning at his midline. Track from your baby's midline to his right side and across his midline to his left side and return to his body's midline. You will notice he can follow a toy horizontally with more awareness of the periphery.

Visual-action song: horizontal tracking

When you sing to your baby, she will watch you with interest. Your little twinkling hand action will capture her attention and encourage visual tracking.

On the floor: Twinkle Twinkle Little Star

Place your baby lying on her back on the floor.

Sit on the floor facing your baby: kneel-sit, or flex and cross your legs over each other, or extend your legs in a v-shape with your baby between your legs. Engage your baby's visual attention by focusing on your baby's face and sing:

Twinkle, twinkle little star
How I wonder what you are?
Up above the world so high
Like a diamond in the sky

Add twinkling hand action.

Bring all your fingers to touch your thumb. With each word, open and close your fingers, like a twinkling star.

Not too fast and not too slow

It may take you a few times to coordinate the pace of your words and hand actions with your baby's ability to track your hand. Notice how fast your hand actions are, and observe your baby. Your baby's tracking may be a little jerky at the beginning.

As you adjust to each other, your baby will begin to regulate the speed of tracking and will soon develop smoother eye movements.

Sing with Actions

Start with your right hand closed— the right distance away is about ten to twelve inches, in line with your baby's visual focus—and engage her attention.

Sing the phrase:

Twinkle, twinkle little star.

Track from your baby's midline to her right side back across her midline to her left side and return to her midline.

Repeat the same movements and sing:

How I wonder what you are?

Observe your baby. Sing the song once and pause.

- Is your baby calm and alert?
- Is she smiling?
- Does she actively move her arms and legs?
- Does she mirror your mouth movements?
- Is she vocalizing and looking at you with anticipation?

Repeat the song. Notice if you and your baby are getting into a smoother tracking rhythm. Singing the song twice may be enough for the first time.

This activity develops attention and listening skills; it encourages both eyes to work together and provides practice in visual tracking and crossing the midline.

Next month we will add the rest of the song and introduce vertical tracking with the words.

● Self-Motivated Learning

Goal-Directed Actions

We know that Isabelle can grasp the smaller spindle in her hand. In this vignette Isabelle is now focused on the flat, wide bar of her bassinette. She turns her head and uses eye-hand coordination, visual attention, touch, and kinesthetic feedback in movement planning to contact the bar.

Visually Directed Reaching

Isabelle extends her right arm and focuses on her right hand touching the side of the bar with her thumb. Her grasp adjusts to the size and shape of the bar. During this action her left arm is flexed and her hand remains closed with her thumb on top of her fingers.

Body Awareness

At the same time babies are exploring their environment, they are learning about themselves and their actions. Isabelle extends and opens her arms sideways in the horizontal dimension. With both hands active, Isabelle brings her thumbs to touch the tips of her index fingers.

Mouthing

Then she flexes her arms and brings her hands together at her midline. With a downward visual gaze she looks at the back of her right hand she is mouthing. The fingertips of her right hand touch the back of her left hand.

Grasping without Looking

Without looking, Isabelle extends her right arm to reach the bar again, shaping her hand to grasp the wide, flat bar between her thumb and fingers.

Her thumb is on one side of the bar and her fingers are on the other side.

Her open right hand moves in concert with her grasp.

Pleasure in Moving

In this uninterrupted playtime, Isabelle now looks up and in a flurry of activity she releases her grasp, moves her arms, opens her hands, and begins kicking her legs.

Resting, she reaches for the adjacent small spindle that she can grasp without looking. Her left hand is closed again with her thumb on top of her fingers.

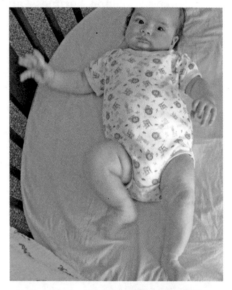

Pleasure in Learning

The vignettes illustrate how babies are learning to learn. In her back-and-forth explorations Isabelle is learning about herself and her environment through her ongoing self-initiated movements and her goal-directed actions. These include:

- Visually directed reaching
- Eye-hand coordination and grasping
- Reaching and grasping without looking.

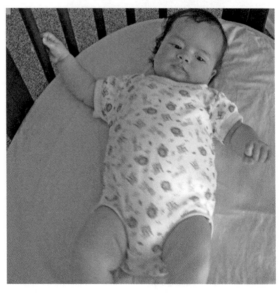

Through patterns of flexion and extension, the kinesthetic and proprioceptive systems inform her about how each part of her body is moving and the relationship of her limbs in space.

Mouthing and self-touch combine in ways so that babies can develop their body awareness, facilitate hand opening, and discriminate their active manual explorations.

The haptic system processes the many different properties of the object she is exploring: size, shape, hardness, and texture through touch and shaping her hand to an object.

Two Month Chapter Review

• • • • •

DEVELOPMENTAL MOVEMENT

- Body awareness: Tactile explorations provide babies with essential information through mouthing, touch, hand-to-hand, and foot-to-foot contact.
- Eye-hand coordination: Eye-hand coordination enhances connections between what your baby feels, touches, and sees within her arm's reach and visual field.
- Mouthing hands: Your baby's lips and fingers are highly sensitive with the highest concentration of touch-receptor cells in the body.
- Waving arms and kicking legs: These movements contribute to your baby's growing kinesthetic awareness.
- Tracking objects: Your baby's eyes are beginning to converge to work together. She can track a toy horizontally with more awareness of the periphery.
- The kinesphere: The kinesphere forms the natural boundary of personal space around the body.

SOCIAL INTERACTION

- Focus: Babies focus in face-to-face interactions with parents and caregivers.
- Social smiling: Smiling is one of the interactive expressions of your two-month-old baby. Babies respond to smiling and elicit smiling in others.
- Body-to-body: Your baby enjoys maintaining hand or foot contact when lying on the floor.

Two Month Chapter Review (cont.)

• • • • •

SELF-MOTIVATED LEARNING

- Reaching and grasping: Visually directed reaching encourages grasping objects.
- Explorations: Explorations include multimodal stimulation promoting kinesthetic, visual, and haptic interactions.
- Actions: Goal-directed actions promote new experiences, perception, and learning.
- Haptic: The baby uses the sense of touch and handling to explore size, shape, hardness, and smoothness of objects.

Month Three

• • • • •

Shaping Movement with Two Hands

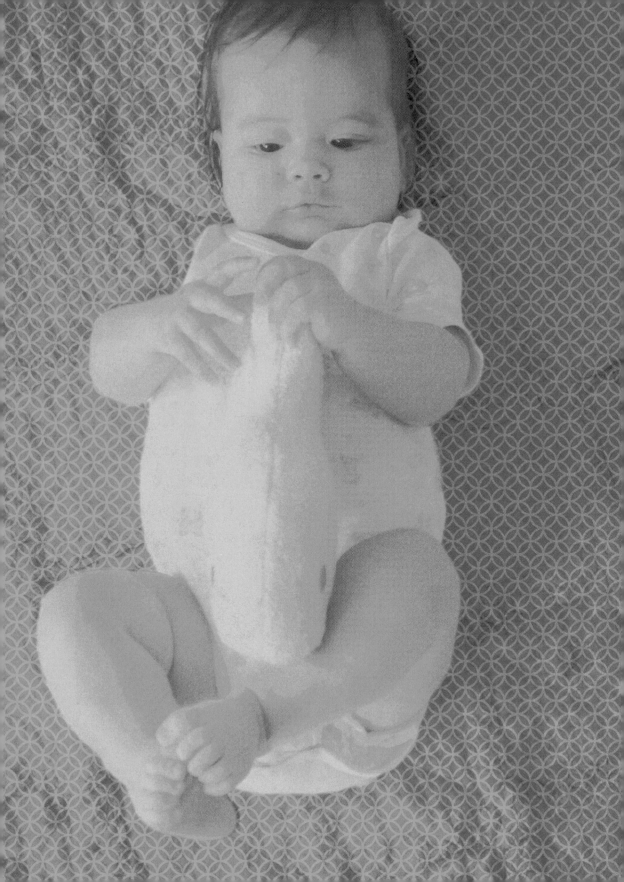

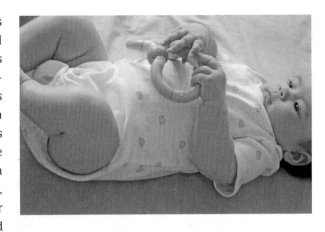

Three-month-old babies are gaining postural control and their actions are becoming more purposeful. Lying on their backs, babies can maintain their heads in midline for longer periods of time. At this age, they are quite content to move within their immediate body space, as defined by the reach of their arms and legs. They can extend and flex their knees and rest their legs in the familiar frog-leg position.

Babies are now more visually aware of their surroundings and watch with keen interest people who move beyond their immediate body space. All the little looks and sounds they make at this age expand their expressive communication skills.

Postural positions are fundamental for toy and object explorations. This month lying in the supine position your baby can bring his hands together at his midline, developing bilateral coordination. This is the ability to use both sides of his body together at the same time.

Handling and exploring toys and objects with both hands and both feet promote the baby's new body awareness explorations. Your baby can explore a lightweight toy or object more easily when lying on his back, by resting the toy on his body.

★ Developmental Movement

Body Awareness

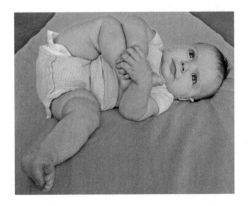

In the supine position, three-month-old babies continue to develop their body awareness within their kinesphere. Kate communicates her physical pleasure by embracing and pressing her foot against her body—and by her delightful smile.

She holds her right foot between her hands, bringing her foot to her midline. Although she opens her mouth wide, she can't quite get her toes to her mouth. But she's already anticipating that possibility.

Rolling onto her back again, Kate kicks her legs and grasps her left foot with her left hand. She turns to focus on her right foot and directs her aim with her right hand to grasp her right foot, demonstrating her developing eye-hand-foot coordination.

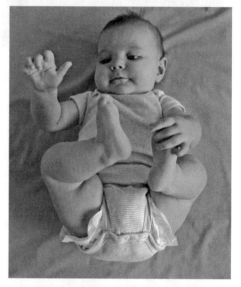

With increased elbow extension and the ability to grasp both feet with their hands, three-month-old babies are able to hold onto their toes.

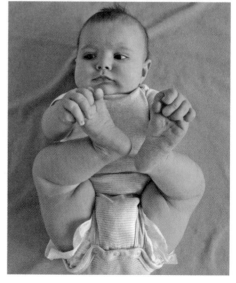

Symmetrical Movement—The Head in Midline

At three months, babies can hold their head in midline for longer periods of time with more bilateral activity. Bilateral coordination is the ability to use both sides of the body together, as this baby does while playing with her stretchy cloth. A self-motivated baby can use many objects for whole body play. Here an everyday stretchy cloth enhances this three-month-old baby's movement development and play exploration.

Babies can maintain their head in midline when lying on their back, tuck their chin, and look down at their hands or the object they are holding between their hands. This is the beginning of visual convergence: a baby's ability to use both eyes together to focus on her hands holding the object.

Bilateral Coordination

Isabelle uses her stretchy cloth to demonstrate her ability to use both sides of her body together. This little cloth is lightweight, small, and stretchy—just the right size. Isabelle holds the cloth between her hands and, interacting with gravity, she raises her feet up off the floor to come into

play by holding onto the other end of the stretchy cloth. Three-month-old babies can also bring their feet together in the familiar frog-leg posture.

Increasing Pressure and Pulling

Holding the cloth with both her hands and gripping the cloth with both feet requires regulating the pressure so it is the same between her hands and between her feet. At the same time she pulls and stretches the cloth—keeping the tension taut—bringing it up to her mouth.

With these movements Isabelle demonstrates a refined kinesthetic sense and tactile awareness—and an increased ability to focus her attention. She knows where each part of her body is and how each part of her body contributes to regulating the amount of pressure and tension needed to hold onto the cloth.

She looks at her hands and pulls the cloth up to touch her lips and begins mouthing it, discriminating between textures and expanding her sensory experience.

Holding a Toy Rattle

If you hold a toy rattle so it lightly touches your baby's navel at the midline, she can grasp and hold it.

Downward visual gaze

Isabelle holds the rattle in one hand and, with a downward visual gaze, begins to shape her other hand to grasp its middle.

Holding the rattle in her right hand, she opens and positions her left hand, touching the narrowest part of the rattle between its two ball shapes. Her thumb touches the rattle under her fingers as she closes her fingers around the middle of the toy to grasp it with her whole hand.

Shaping Hands to Toys

The best time to introduce a rattle to a baby is at three months when she is beginning to shape her hands to toys and objects. Her fingers are in a typical grasp position and she begins to transfer the toy back and forth, in hand-to-hand play. The baby also has the ability to open her hand and let the rattle fall out.

Matching What She Hears with What She Sees

The middle part of the rattle is clear so the baby can see the colorful beads inside it and match the soft tinkling sounds she hears with the movement of the beads she sees.

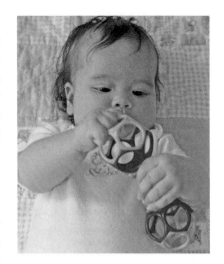

♥ Social Interaction

Parent-Baby Activities

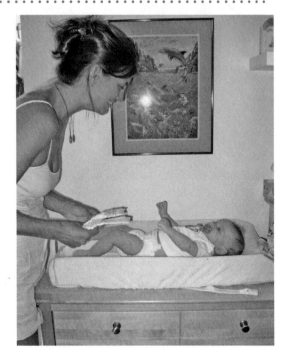

Body Awareness

In the first few months while holding your baby in your arms, you engage your baby in face-to-face activities; you can also do these activities on the floor with your baby, or even at the diapering table. You are expanding your baby's body awareness by touching and naming the parts of his body he is exploring.

Body-naming game

When your baby is lying on his back, position yourself so you can observe what he is doing. In a singsong voice, engage your baby in a little body game that goes like this:

- Touch one part of your baby's body he is discovering such as his hands.

- You can say: "I see you've found your hands today."

- Then say, "I see you've found your feet."

- With a soft touch, circle your baby's belly button and say, "Here is (your baby's name) belly button, round and round it goes."

Parents and babies enjoy these belly-button action songs that reinforce their baby's body-awareness explorations. As you sing, watch his excitement spread from his navel through his whole body.

You can continue this exploration, as your baby expands his body awareness and adds new tactile movement explorations each month. For example at four months say: "I see you've found your knees today." And at five months, "I see you've found your toes today."

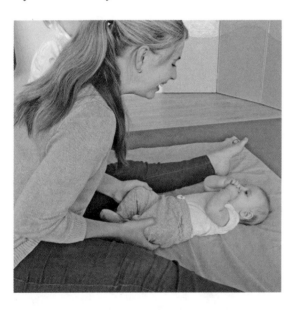

Body Positions on the Floor

The following body-position tips for you and your baby can be used for social play, tracking activities, nursery rhymes, and playing with toys. It is helpful to offer three-month-old babies appropriate-sized objects and toys that enhance their symmetrical explorations, mid-line development, and downward visual gaze.

Place your baby on the floor lying on his back. Sit centered in front of your baby: kneel-sit, sit with both legs to one side, cross your legs, or extend your legs in a v-shape with your baby between your legs. Engage your baby's visual attention by looking at him and smiling.

Action Songs for Visual Tracking

Three-month-old babies are beginning to track more smoothly in the horizontal and vertical dimensions. The following are three play activities to encourage your baby's visual tracking development. When doing these activities, move your hands, small toy, or object at an even pace—not too fast and not too slow. This will encourage your baby to track with smooth eye movements. I also include a movement activity to introduce diagonal tracking.

Twinkle Twinkle Little Star: horizontal and vertical tracking

Place your baby lying on her back on the floor. Sit centered in front of your baby: kneel-sit, both legs to one side, cross your legs, or extend your legs in a v-shape with your baby between your legs.

Engage your baby's attention by focusing on your baby's face and singing:

Twinkle, twinkle little star
How I wonder what you are
Up above the world so high
Like a diamond in the sky
Twinkle, twinkle little star
How I wonder what you are.

Add twinkling hand actions

With your right hand, bring all your fingers to touch your thumb. With each word, open and close your fingers, like a twinkling star.

Horizontal tracking

Track from your baby's midline to her right side, back across her midline to her left side, and return to her midline.

Sing:

Twinkle, twinkle little star.

Move from her midline to her left side and back across midline and sing:

How I wonder what you are?

Track from your baby's midline to her right side and back to her midline.

Vertical tracking: up toward the ceiling

Vertical tracking up: Begin by extending your right arm and index finger in an upward direction toward the ceiling while singing.

Up above the world so high

Continue with one hand or add the following variation.

Two hands together

Bring your hands together and make a diamond shape with your index fingers and thumbs.

Vertical tracking: down toward the floor

Vertical tracking down: Begin flexing both arms as you bring your hands in a diamond shape down while singing:

Like a diamond in the sky.

Add twinkling hand actions

With your right hand, bring all your fingers to touch your thumb. With each word, open and close your fingers, like a twinkling star.

Repeat horizontal tracking with the words as you did at the beginning of the song.

Hickory Dickory Dock: horizontal and vertical tracking

Engage your baby by smiling and tell her, "We're going to sing Hickory Dickory Dock."

Horizontal tracking

Extend your right index finger.

From your baby's midline move smoothly to your baby's right side and across the midline to the left side; continue moving to the baby's midline.

In a sing-song voice say:

Hickory, dickory, dock.

Vertical tracking: up toward the ceiling

Walk index and middle fingers together. Continue adding new vocal tones.

The mouse ran up the clock.

At the top say:

The clock struck one.

Extend your index finger. Walk two fingers together, index and middle finger tracking downward, and say:

The mouse ran down.

Horizontal tracking

Extend your right index finger.
   Repeat: Track horizontally from your baby's midline, move smoothly to her right side and back across to her left side, and return to her midline.

Hickory, dickory, dock.

Two Little Birds Hopping and Flying: diagonal tracking on both sides

Introduce diagonal tracking at the end of this month or next month. Engage your baby by smiling and tell her: "I'm going to sing a little song for you. This song is about: two little birds hopping on the ground and flying up into the sky. One bird's name is Polly and one is called Paul."
   Place your fingertips lightly on your baby's navel at her midline.
   In a singsong voice say:

Two little birds hopping on the ground, one named Polly and one named Paul.

Right Hand: Move your right hand in a diagonal line, fluttering your fingers like the wings of a bird and continue in a singsong voice:

Fly away Polly, and Polly flew this way.

Move your right hand on the diagonal upward.

Left Hand: Move your left hand on a diagonal from your baby's midline, fluttering your fingers like the wings of a bird and in a sing-song voice continue:

Fly away Paul, and Paul flew that way.

With both your arms in a v-shape—pause.

Both flew together high up in the sky.

Move your arms from the v-shape to vertical. With your right hand fluttering, bring your hand down to your baby's navel and sing:

Right hand: *Polly flew down.*
Left Hand: *Paul flew down.*

Together they hopped right into town.

These action songs provide you with specific information about your baby's eye-tracking movements and directions. They encourage your movement and observation skills as you pay close attention to the timing of your arm and hand actions.

To begin, you may just engage your baby with one little song and repeat it in a few days, before adding a new song and action. What is most important is your focus on your baby, your mutual attention to the song, and you and your baby's enjoyment together.

● Self-Motivated Learning

A Baby Grasps Her Soft Toy Whale

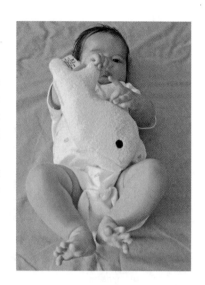

One afternoon Isabelle plays briefly with her soft toy whale. She grasps one side of the tail in her right hand and points to the tail with her left extended index finger.

She then moves on to explore her hands and is able to bring both hands together, matching her fingers and thumbs.

Matching Fingers and Thumbs

We've already learned how a three-month-old baby coordinates her two sides by bringing her hands and feet together in bilateral play and how she handles a small toy rattle.

In this vignette we marvel at how Isabelle refines her fine motor skills by articulating her fingers of both hands and matching them together.

Body Awareness

Visual processing, movement, and finger-to-finger contact inform the part of the body she is exploring and increase her body awareness.

Bimanual Coordination

As bimanual coordination develops, babies use both hands together. In this documented sequence Isabelle matches up the fingers of one hand with the corresponding fingers of the other.

Shaping Movement with Two Hands **51**

Finger Articulation

The fingertips are highly sensitive to touch. Finger articulation is the ability to move each finger, one at a time. Isabelle explores her fingers, touching the tip of each one with a precise, light contact.

The Precision Side of the Hand

Is there a specific organization she uses to match up her fingers and thumbs?

The thumb, index, and middle fingers are described as the precision side of the hand that children use in many activities.

Isabelle's ability to regulate her attention while focusing on her hand and finger explorations develops her fine motor control and articulation.

This capability enables babies to coordinate their hands together to investigate toys and objects using a precision grip.

It is also the foundation for developing functional skills like holding a spoon to feed herself, coloring with a crayon, holding a paint brush, and playing a musical instrument.

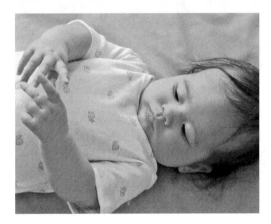

A Baby Explores Handling Her Toy Whale

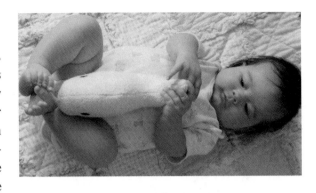

The next day Isabelle continues to actively explore her soft toy whale. She holds the toy at her body's midline aligned between her hands and feet. She experiences the size and weight of the toy on her whole body, and the rough textured fabric is stimulating to her hands, bare legs, and feet. She grasps and squeezes the whale's tail with her left hand. Flexing her chin, she gazes downward while articulating her left index finger.

Left Index Finger on Right

Grasping a toy and matching fingers, Isabelle pulls the whale upright and looks at her left index finger that rests on top of the middle finger of her right hand.

Orienting Her Right Hand

Looking at her left hand and holding onto the whale's tail, she extends all her fingers and orients her right hand to contact the other side of the forked tail.

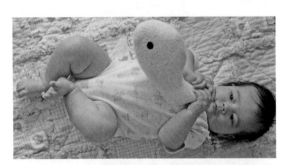

Right Index Finger on Left

Raising her right leg up off the floor, she supports the whale on her body and left leg. She has now extended her right index finger, which she places on top of her left index finger.

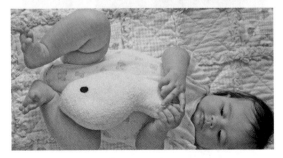

Shaping Movement with Two Hands **53**

Grasping the Forked-Tail Fin

Isabelle uses both hands to hold onto each side of the whale's tail fin. But now it is the toy's tag on the tail fin that captures her attention, and she touches the tag with her right index finger.

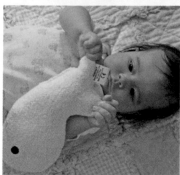

Focusing on the Tag

She focuses on the tag that is on the right forked-tail fin.

Shifting Focus

She shifts her focus from the tag on the right side of the tail to her left hand; holding the opposite tail fin she looks at her thumb that is covering her index finger.

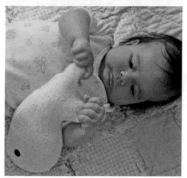

Right Index Finger on the Tag

Isabelle shifts her gaze back to her right hand and focuses on her right index finger, touching the tag on the fin.

Visual and Tactile Body Exploration with Her Whale

Isabelle turns her head farther and holds onto the toy whale with one hand. Now, she looks at her toy from a new perspective.

Because the whale's tail fin is v-shaped and the toy is lightweight, Isabelle can grasp it easily in one hand and hold it up by the tail.

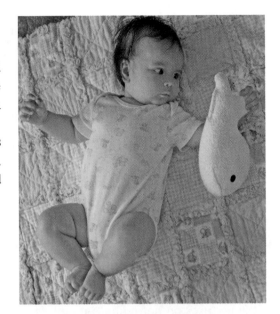

Sensing the Back of Her Hand

With her toy whale lying beside her on the floor, Isabelle looks at the curved shape of the whale's back and tail. She uses this visual information and softly flexes her fingers, shaping her hand to snuggle deeply into the arc of the whale's tail. Active exploration of the whale through touch stimulates the skin's surface of her fingers and the back of her hand.

Shaping Her Hand to the Whale's Tail

Isabelle notices that her whale is in a new position, and she makes a slight adjustment in the position of her arm. She flexes her elbow more so that her hand nestles into the shaped curve again.

Resting Her Hand on the Whale's Head

Isabelle lowers her legs and feet onto the floor. Notice her whale is now in a different position, facing the left side of her body. She extends her arm sideways and rests her arm and palm of her hand on top of her whale's head. She extends her fingers, touching the place she was exploring with the back of her hand.

Sensing Her Arm and Hand

She releases her contact and explores the textures on her quilt. The quilt is fuzzy and smooth, and softer than the rough-texture of her toy whale.

Resting Her Hand on the Whale's Tail

Isabelle pushes the top of the whale with her hand, and the whale ends up in a new position, facing downward. She rests her hand on her whale's tail.

Notice Isabelle's calm gaze; her deepening relaxation is expressed by extending her legs and the way she spreads her arms to rest on the floor.

After watching Isabelle's explorations—that she initiated and completed at her own pace—we can appreciate her contentment.

Let's look at what Isabelle was learning in her self-directed play explorations.

Multimodal Learning

The baby's multimodal learning experiences obtained through exploring toys and objects include vision, hearing, touch, and kinesthetic stimulation for perceiving information in the environment. When different sensory neurons respond to stimuli, they send differing messages to the central nervous system.

The Sense of Touch

We receive tactile information from the sensory receptors in the skin over our entire body. But the tactile sense is more than just a passive receiver of information—it is through active touch that we explore and learn about our environment. Lying on the floor on a textured quilt Isabelle experiences the floor as hard, the quilt as soft, smooth, and its tufts of fabric as fuzzy. She contacts the textured toy whale with different parts of her body, and her bare arms and legs experience the rough texture.

Tactile and Cutaneous Inputs

When the baby's hand initially contacts an object, the information is provided by the touch receptors in the skin. The receptors provide information about the object, such as texture and hardness. This information is tactile and cutaneous. When the hand applies force to hold onto an object, information about the position and motion of the hand in relationship to the object comes into play. The sensing and actions performed are referred to as active touch.

Kinesthetic Inputs

As Isabelle explores the whale in relationship to her own body, she develops an awareness of her body in motion and where each limb is in relationship to the other. She also discovers new tactile information about the size, shape, weight, and texture of her toy whale. These experiences form the foundation of a baby's ability to match what she sees with what she experiences—by looking, touching, grasping, mouthing, and handling.

Three-Dimensional Experience

When she shapes her hand and arm to her toy whale, she notices these specific sensations and perceives a three-dimensional awareness of her hand and arm. At the same time she is receiving information about the size and three-dimensional shape of the toy whale she is actively exploring.

In this vignette you have learned about two aspects of haptic experience: the special tactile properties and curved contour shape of the toy.

Size and Weight

Although the size of the toy whale seems relatively large, this lightweight toy is easy to grasp and hold while resting it on her body. Through handling and manipulating the toy, Isabelle receives information about its size, weight, and texture. The kinesthetic sense helps Isabelle monitor the effort needed to move and handle the toy so she can continue exploring her whale.

Shaping Her Hand to the Shape of the Toy

Shape perception also reflects the haptic inputs of the hand to the curved shape of the object. The contoured shape is convex and the complementary shape of her hand fits into the curvature of the whale's tail.

Pleasure in Play

Integrating all her learning experiences, Isabelle expresses her pleasure in her play interactions with her toy whale through the calm, contented look on her face, and her relaxed body posture.

Rolling: Supine to Side Lying

When babies rotate their head to the side, the neck righting reaction can still cause them to roll over onto their side.

With simultaneous hip and knee flexion, Kate raises her legs higher and holds onto her ankle and foot.

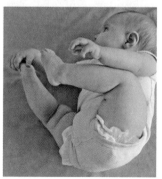

Rolling to side lying begins from a symmetrical flexed posture and is important for both visual and vestibular development.

As she gains momentum and rolls onto her right side, she lets go of her legs.

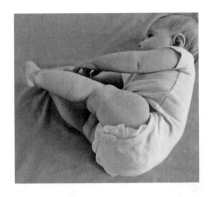

Kate can roll to both sides. When babies lie on one side of their body, the weight-bearing side receives new tactile information. Kate actively extends her elbows and knees.

Baby Moves in Tummy Time

Kate lies on her front, in the prone position, for tummy-time play. Although prone is not a functional play position for babies yet, Kate is beginning to bring her hands together in midline and can maintain this position for short periods of time.

With improved head control and increased spinal extension developing from the head downwards, her pelvis moves closer to the floor. Lifting her chest higher, Kate begins to support herself on her forearms.

Three-month-old babies are more visually aware of their environment. Kate's focus is on the soft plushy toy in front of her. Her interest in reaching the toy can be seen in the flexion of her left leg that is ready to push off to extend her leg to move closer to the soft toy.

Shaping Movement with Two Hands **59**

Kate will be exploring these movements over and over in the next few months. Your baby's ability to tuck her chin when she's in the prone position is a significant development for all her visual-play explorations.

Tummy Time: Body-to-Body

Rolling Your Baby onto Your Body

Lying beside your baby, roll your baby over on top of your body. In this position you feel his little hands gently push against you. When you add soft humming sounds, your baby will feel sound vibrations coming from your chest that will soothe him.

Social Play

In this body-to-body position, your baby can touch, smile, and engage with you in social play. At the same time, these pleasant body-to-body interactions help your baby become more comfortable on his tummy.

Three Month Chapter Review

• • • • •

DEVELOPMENTAL MOVEMENT

- Body awareness: Your baby is developing tactile explorations in the supine position: hand-to-hand, foot-to-foot and one hand holding one foot.
- Supine position: Symmetry and midline development leads to more bilateral activity.
- Grasping: Grasping different objects generates new hand-shaping movements.
- Bilateral coordination: Your baby's ability to use both sides of the body together at the same time.

SOCIAL INTERACTION

- Action songs: Action songs develop horizontal, vertical, and diagonal tracking.
- Body awareness games: These games reinforce the baby's body awareness explorations.
- Body-to-body: This position encourages body comfort in tummy-time play.
- Cuddles and touching: Your baby cuddles and reaches with both hands to touch you.
- Expressive communication: Your baby cries less, laughs out loud, and vocalizes more.

Three Month Chapter Review (cont.)

● ○ ● ● ○

SELF-MOTIVATED LEARNING

- Hand-to-hand: The baby matches her hands and fingers in the supine position.
- Haptic: The baby learns to recognize properties of objects through handling.
- Action: Goal-directed actions with toys and objects in the environment lead to new experiences and learning.
- Exploring three-dimensional toys: The baby matches and shapes her hand with the shape of a toy.

Month Four

• • • • •

Goal-Directed Actions and Gestures

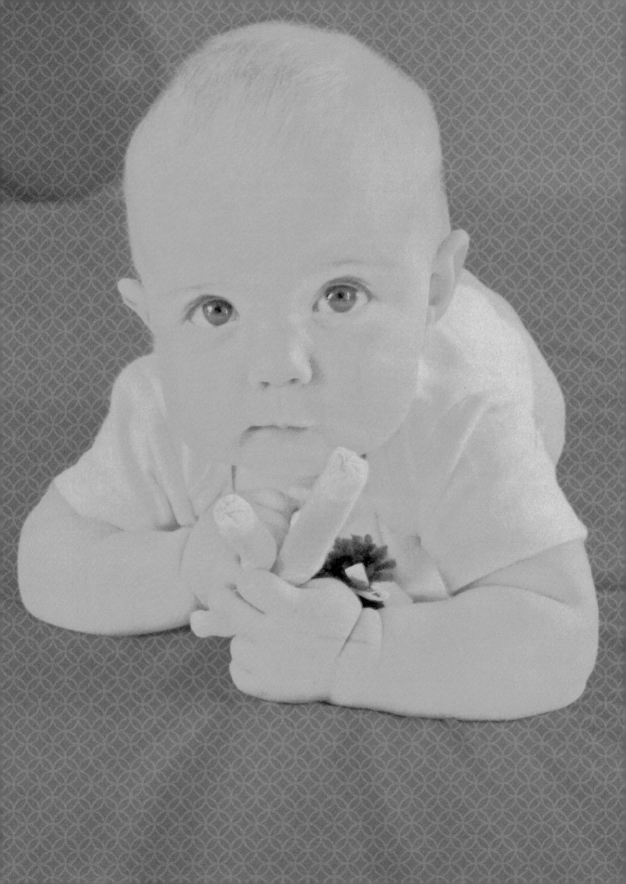

At four months, in the prone position your baby can maintain her head at a 90-degree angle in midline. By keeping her head in midline, she can coordinate both sides of her body, bring her hands together, and look down at her hands to participate in purposeful play and tactile explorations. The coordination she is developing in eye-hand explorations is a result of her improved ability to maintain head control, especially the ability to tuck her chin (head flexion) to look down at her hands.

Exploring what they can do with a toy in the prone position, babies expand their problem-solving strategies. Although four-month-old babies can grasp a toy within reach and handle the toy with both hands, reaching out for a toy with one hand is not yet within their developmental-movement repertoire.

As you expand your observation skills, you will notice all the little cues and signals your baby is communicating. This month we discover that four-month-old babies lying in the supine position can use the pointing gesture to communicate. The baby's expressive gesture can now be used to direct an adult's attention to objects the baby is exploring in her surroundings.

In uninterrupted play, babies actively choose what they will focus on. This month babies regulate their attention and develop action plans to reach their goal. You have already learned that a baby's exploration of toys is not limited to simple grasping; they can handle toys and objects in intentional ways that prompts them to go further. Curiosity, interest, problem-solving skills, and discoveries through play—these are the qualities she'll build on for all her future learning.

★ Developmental Movement

Symmetrical-Push Patterns

When your baby is in the prone position, she can support herself on her forearms. You'll become familiar with the symmetrical-movement patterns as playing on her tummy becomes a functional play position.

Symmetrical-Movement Patterns: Upper and Lower Body

Symmetrical-movement patterns differentiate and integrate the upper and lower body and develop midline alignment. This creates the symmetrical foundation for your baby to develop integrated postures, binocular vision, and the ability to cross the body's midline.

The symmetrical-push patterns are based on the baby's developing spinal patterns that provide the body's internal core support. The four-month-old baby has developed the strength and control to support herself on her forearms.

Spinal-Movement Patterns

Spinal movements differentiate the front of the body from the back of our body and develop an integrated spinal axis. They provide the internal core support for your baby to begin to coordinate her arms and legs in relationship to each other and in relationship to her whole body. Spinal-movement patterns establish the baby's head-to-tail connection in all four body positions—lying on her back, front, and each side.

When your four-month-old baby is lying on her front, she can extend and flex her head. Lying on her back, she begins to lift and flex her head. She may lift up her head, for example, to watch a belly-button game.

Your Baby's Shapely Neck Curve

Your baby's neck curve is developed through body movement in the prone position. From the primary c-curve shape of the spine, the first of the secondary curves to develop is the neck curve, called the cervical curve.

Cervical curve develops in tummy time

Your baby's antigravity movements—lifting, turning, extending, and flexing his head in the prone position—develop the shapely neck curve. Tummy-time activities provide your baby the ability to coordinate these spinal movements for good head and neck control, and postural alignment.

Body Awareness

You have been learning about the close link between body movement, touch, and visual processing that informs babies about themselves from the beginning.

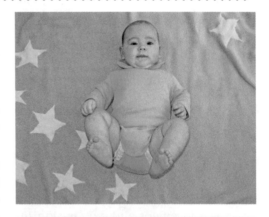

At each stage of development babies learn about their body through their movement and tactile explorations. Exploring new body connections and new movement skills, babies expand an awareness of their body on all four sides: lying on their back, lying on their front, and lying on each side

To encourage your baby's body awareness explorations on the floor give your baby:

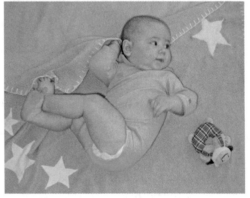

- opportunities to move and explore with bare legs and feet.

- time to explore tactile sensations in developing new body-to-body connections.

Overuse of Baby Containers

Think about all the products that inhibit a baby's freedom to move. Parents and caregivers can make informed decisions about the use of baby containers when they learn about the importance of their baby's body awareness, movement patterns, and self-produced actions that enhance their baby's social and cognitive development.

Overuse of infant seats, swings, exercise saucers, and baby bouncers limits your baby's interactions with gravity and natural movement development.

- Infant car seats: Note I am *not* referring to car seats that are essential for your baby's safety and must be used at *all* times.

Overuse of infant seats and baby swings:

- Inhibits spinal movement and active visual exploration.

- Prevents four- to six-month-old babies in the prone position from weight bearing on their forearms and weight shifting which are necessary for reaching.

- Inhibits development of muscle strength, balance, and coordination.

Overuse of exercise saucers and baby bouncers:

- Inhibits a baby's spinal development in prone, supine, and side-lying positions.

- Leads a baby to support his body weight on his feet before independent standing.

- Holds a baby in the upright position, preventing age-appropriate movement and exploration in the supine, prone, and side-lying positions.

Bumbo seats are not safe for babies. Babies will learn to sit independently on their own. As for walkers, it is now commonly known that walkers pose a potential risk and can be dangerous if babies are left unattended in them. Walkers prevent development of a baby's postural control in weight shifting when walking. They encourage mobility beyond the baby's natural motor development.

Body Awareness Essentials

In the supine position, Kaya flexes her knees, lifting both feet up off the floor. This strengthens the symmetrical-movement patterns and midline orientation she is developing.

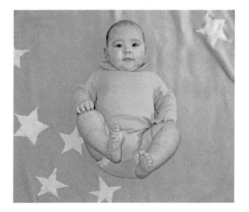

Centering her head in midline, Kaya coordinates her upper and lower body together. As she interacts with gravity, Kaya learns more about how her body moves. What body connections is she making?

Kaya flexes both legs together and extends both arms together to reach down and touch her knees with her hands, increasing her tactile body awareness. She senses how each part of her body is moving, the relationship of her arms and legs to each other, and where each part is in space.

Notice how your baby's movement organization has progressed from the simple flexion and extension patterns of your two-month-old baby.

Visual Processing

Looking Sideways

Four-month-old babies are visually active and interested in their surroundings. Their visual control has developed so that they can now smoothly track a moving object horizontally from one side to the other. With increased head control, babies can turn their head to either side and can move their eyes independently to see farther.

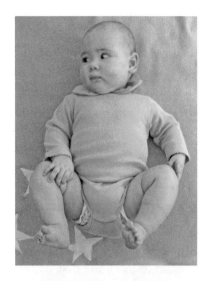

As Kaya explores her body, she senses the different parts of her legs that she is touching with her hands and fingers. These explorations are fundamental to the way babies embody themselves and develop an awareness of their body's boundaries.

Looking Downward

In the supine position, Kaya can turn her head in all directions. She has greater control of her eye movements, and the range of her visual field is expanding. Every time Kaya is placed on her special blanket to play, she looks to locate where the stars are in relationship to the position of her body.

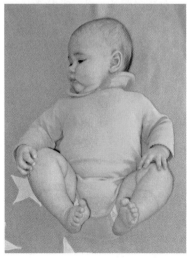

She can look upward when the star is above her head. She can turn her head to each side to look at the stars on both sides of her body. As she turns her head to the right, she flexes her chin to look downward at the cluster of stars.

Kaya reaches down in a typical four-month-old position with both hands on her knees.

Rolling Over: Tracking the Index Finger

This sequence shows how a four-month-old baby rolls over from lying on her back to her side and over into the prone position. Turning her head to look at her hand, she visually tracks her index finger to move and change her place in space. Rolling over from back to front is a spinal-movement pattern that often begins with head rotation.

Her eye-hand coordination directs the movement pathway in rolling over. Reaching with her arm and leg across her body, Isabel's eyes are focused on her closed hand that initiates the movement. She begins rolling onto her side.

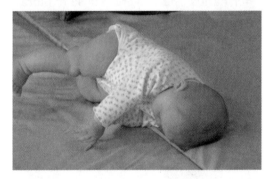

As she focuses on her hand, she opens it and touches the mat with the tip of her index finger. Isabel initiates the action by visually tracking her hand while rolling over onto the front of her body.

In the prone position with her arm resting on the mat, she closes her hand and focuses on her extended index finger. When she completes her exhilarating movement, she looks up; her delightful smile communicates her pleasure in reaching this new body position and perspective of her surroundings.

A baby's movement organization in rolling over from her back onto her front evolves over several months:

Three-month-old babies explore primitive log rolling to side lying.

Four-month-old babies often begin rolling over to side lying from a flexed posture with hips and knees flexed and hands on their knees.

Lying on the floor and positioning yourself to each side of your baby, you have been encouraging your baby to lift and turn his head in both directions. Head rotation often initiates rolling over to side lying. Now you are encouraging your baby to roll over to side lying on both sides. This movement enhances your baby's visual processing; vestibular, tactile, and proprioceptive feedback; and muscle balance, equally on both sides of the body.

Babies typically begin rolling over from back to front any time between four and five months, but each baby is unique, and develops in her own rhythm and timing.

Index Finger—Mouthing, Movement, and Gesture

This is an introduction to understanding your baby's preverbal communication in social interactions. During this month you have been learning how babies explore the close links between their own movement, touch, and visual processing in developing their body awareness. Babies' antigravity movements and body explorations are fundamental to how they embody themselves. Babies explore mouthing their index finger, and the actions of isolating and extending their index finger, before they are able to use the pointing gesture in their expressive communication. Let's review two earlier explorations.

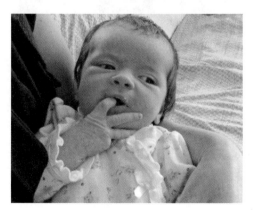

Mouthing

Mouthing their hands, newborn babies suck their thumbs and fingers. When your baby is awake, you may notice her isolating, extending, and mouthing her index finger. She can do this with both hands.

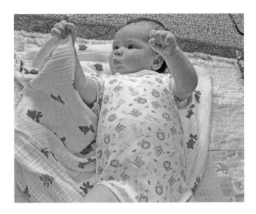

Extending Her Arm and Index Finger

Lying in the supine position, this two-and-half-month old grasps her blanket, focuses on her index finger that is positioned on top of her thumb, and isolates and extends her index finger; at the same time she extends her arm above her.

In a natural setting four-month-old babies explore objects and expressively communicate when lying in either the supine or prone position.

Pointing and Smiling

How do four-month-old babies play with familiar toys and everyday objects in ways that produce novel experiences during their explorations? How do they explore their immediate surroundings? These questions lead us to the broader question: how do preverbal babies expressively communicate to themselves? While playing on the floor, babies act spontaneously and expressively respond to their actions. A baby may make a clicking sound with her mouth, or a scratching sound by raking a textured carpet, that she finds funny. These novel sensations and sounds may cause her to smile at her own actions. In this play session we see an example of a baby interacting with her toy by pointing and smiling.

Playing with her toy rattle, a four-month-old baby is developing her fine motor skills and hand movements in the prone position. She points to the smiley face on the yellow bead that she recognizes and is familiar with in her everyday play explorations.

To understand the meaning in movement during this preverbal stage, we emphasize paying attention to the baby's expressive communication cues—his body position, posture, and gestures.

Communicating in these early months is a subtle nonverbal dialogue between parent and baby that builds close communication bonds. Understanding what babies are capable of encourages responsive parenting in your parent-baby social interactions.

Laughing, this expressive two-month-old baby extends his arm and index finger.

Not only does every play exploration take place in a developmental position but expressive communication also takes place in postural positions in relationship to the parent or caregiver.

When you tune into your baby's body language you will notice these subtle preverbal communication cues that begin early. We have already learned how babies shift their gaze, expressively communicate through their whole body, and rhythmically use hand gestures interacting with an adult. Babies can self-regulate stimulation by averting their gaze and looking away to integrate their experience. Responsive parents who are tuned into their baby's preverbal signals will recognize the need to tone down stimulation before their baby is over-stimulated, even if the stimulation is initially positive.

The following Baby Star sequence is about a four-month-old baby lying on her starry blanket on the floor, as she does every day. What is new and what I would like to bring attention to in this vignette is the importance of observing babies in natural body positions at their developmental-movement level. In this vignette, Kaya is lying on her back in the supine position: we notice she wants to share something about the blanket she is lying on.

An older child who wants to share something would just point to the star and say, "Look at the stars on my blanket." The broader question is: "When do babies become intentional in their communication?" Until recently, it was commonly assumed that the pointing gesture develops after independent sitting, and before this time infants aren't aware of their communication signals.

However, babies are communicating with parents and caregivers through their focus, posture, and gestures even by four months. Knowing this is important so that you can support and facilitate your baby's preverbal communication that enhances your social interactions together.

♥ Social Interaction

Intentional Preverbal Communication

Four-month-old babies can lead a social interaction by directing attention to objects they are familiar with and interested in. In movement play Kaya explores her starry blanket every day.

Sharing Attention

To understand the meaning of Kaya's focus of attention, we look at her body position and movement development.

Lying on her blanket in the supine position, with her head centered in midline, her legs are flexed with her left hand on her left knee. Kaya looks directly at me while she signals with her right arm that she is interested in something else. I am looking at Kaya and smiling—my expressive response lets her know I am paying attention to her and her actions.

Intentional Gestures

What is extraordinary is that this four-month-old baby is inviting me to look in the direction she is pointing. Kaya spreads her right arm sideways. Babies open their arms to the side to locate people or objects in the environment. Looking more closely at the horizontal direction of her arm, we notice she is extending her index finger and is pointing to a specific area on her blanket. What is Kaya showing me?

Kaya is pointing to the group of white stars clustered together on the right side of her blue blanket. Kaya's focus and gesture expressively communicate what she wants to share with me. When a baby points with her index finger, she initiates and directs the interaction. She selects the object she is interested in and with a pointing gesture directs the adult's attention to the selected object. Her direct focus and pointing gesture guide my attention to the cluster of white stars on her blue blanket.

Kaya's gesture illustrates a more complex concept of pointing with the index finger as an expressive communication gesture called "declarative pointing," which means a gesture that shows something to someone else.

Social Cooperation

Pointing in this example doesn't mean that this four-month-old wants a specific toy or object. By pointing to the stars on her blanket, Kaya communicates that she is sharing something she knows intimately through her experience of being on her starry blanket every day. We can assume that by pointing to the stars on her blanket that she likes the stars and, being responsive to me, she wants me to look at the stars too.

In the discussion of their research work on cortical activation in young infants, Sarah Lloyd-Fox at the Centre for Brain and Cognitive Development at the University of London and her colleagues report that infants use their hands both to touch and explore their environment, and also to gesture to communicate information socially.[1]

And these little gestures can be so easily overlooked, which means a baby then misses out on being able to take the lead in a social interaction with you and share an everyday experience that has meaning to her. When you or your caregiver set time aside to patiently observe your baby every day, your baby will engage you in her new explorations and you will expand your social repertoire together.

In this next Baby Star vignette Kaya focuses her attention directly on one star.

The importance of these explorations is that they are motivated and directed by the baby. Through her everyday play experiences Kaya is learning to distinguish between the many small stars clustered together and one large star. What adds to the complexity of her learning is her changing orientation to the stars on the blanket.

Kaya moves on her blanket every day with her body in a different spatial relationship to the stars. Next, through her focus, movement, and problem-solving skills she develops an action plan and moves her body to reach her one special star.

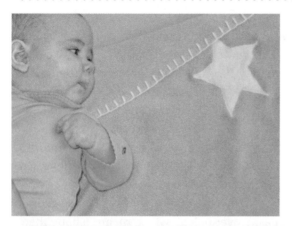

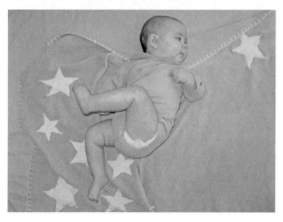

Looking at My Big Star

In the beginning of this sequence Kaya is exploring a larger spatial area on her blanket. Kaya turns her head farther to look at her big white star. A little smile glimmers. Her smile—a subtle expressive-communication cue—lets us know something else is going to happen.

With a little body twist she extends her right arm to grasp her left foot. In this position look what Kaya can do. She holds onto her toes with her finger tips—adjusting her grasp and finger pressure.

A Star Action Plan

Pressing her lips together, Kaya focuses more intently on her big white star.

She perks up! Then she lets go of her toes.

She has an action plan in mind. How do we know this? Because of what happens next!

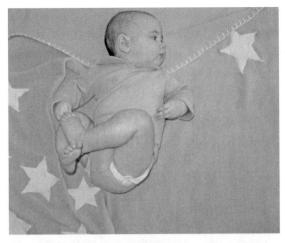

Focusing on My Star

With her focus of attention on the big white star, Kaya brings her legs closer together again. She touches the left side of her body with her fingertips and holds her right knee with her right hand.

When planning the next move, a baby actively focuses on the toy or object of interest.

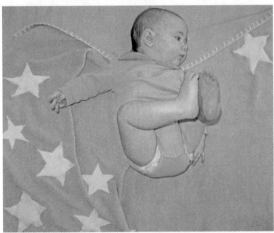

Body in Motion

With a little head flexion, Kaya looks downward away from her big white star. Four-month-old babies can symmetrically flex their hips and knees and bring their feet together to roll onto their side.

Rolling over with head flexion encourages control of her downward visual gaze and visual convergence. Therefore, rolling with head flexion, rather than head extension, is a more integrated movement when rolling to the side-lying position.

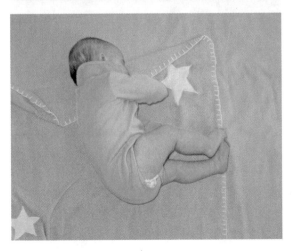

Pathway to My Star

Kaya wants to get closer to the one big white star. She reaches across her body with her right arm, which helps her to roll over to get closer to her star.

Lying on her side is a more dynamic position for a baby. In this position both legs are symmetrically flexed. By the end of the fourth month, babies may begin to separate their legs from each other, creating more options for new coordinated movements. We saw this when Isabel rolled over from her back to her front.

In the side-lying position, four-month-old babies still rest their head on the floor when playing with a toy or, as in Kaya's case, to see something close up. Kaya singles out one star with an expressive gesture that seems to say, "This is my favorite star!"

Touching My Star

Kaya doesn't just want to look at her star; she wants to touch it. During this month your four-month-old baby continues to explore different textures and surfaces that stimulate her tactile awareness.

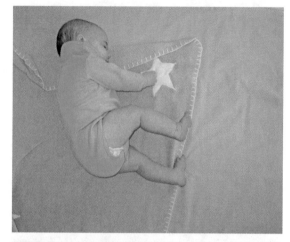

Touching her big, soft fuzzy star on her blanket feels different than when Kaya rakes a textured carpet with her fingers, or squeezes a squishy toy in the bathtub. Each tactile exploration sends a different sensory message to the baby's developing nervous system that stimulates her brain development.

Rolling on Top of My Star

Kaya practices tummy time with her mother every day. During a baby's first explorations rolling over from her back onto her tummy, her hand can sometimes get stuck underneath her body.

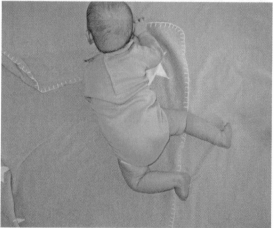

Kaya's mother knows her baby can organize her body and move her arm by herself. She observes patiently, while Kaya frees her arm so she can support herself on both forearms. When you see your baby as a self-motivated learner, you will calmly give your baby sufficient time to organize her body by herself.

Your baby's experience when lying on her side and rolling over is vital because it activates many body systems: tactile, visual, vestibular, and kinesthetic senses.

Bright Eyes Twinkling

How does a four-month-old baby expressively communicate her mastery to an adult? With bright eyes twinkling and a beaming face! Kaya shares her pleasure in her dynamic experiences: she did what she intended to do. When babies carry out their action plans, they develop self-confidence and pleasure in directing their experiences—learning to move from motivation to mastery.

Kaya can't verbally tell us how she developed her action plan, but through developing your keen observation skills you know:

- Her motivation was to reach her one big star.

- She developed a goal-directed action plan.

- She communicated her pleasure by her bright eyes and beaming face.

Where Did My Star Go?

At the end of the play session, her mother notices that Kaya's arm ruffles and folds the blanket so that it hides the one big star. For a four-month-old baby this is an unexpected and puzzling event.

Before we can wonder how Kaya perceives this experience, we observe to see whether she can move to uncover the star. Because she isn't supporting herself on both forearms she can't shift her weight yet to support herself on one side— which would allow her to reach forward with the opposite arm to uncover the star. She won't be able to do this until next month, when five-month-olds typically organize and integrate the lateral-movement patterns.

Kaya's mother can uncover the star and show Kaya the star

is still there, but a four-month-old baby may not grasp this meaning. In a few months Kaya will learn what disappears can reappear. Understanding the concept of object permanence will take more experience—through games like peek-a-boo, hide-and-seek, and looking for toys that disappear behind furniture in her environment.

What is most important for Kaya now is that through her experience of rolling over on top of her star she begins to understand the concept of over and under.

Developing Concepts on Her Starry Blanket

Kaya's starry blanket, which introduced her to the one-star and many-stars concept, demonstrates a number of other qualities such as color, shape, size, space, texture, and numbers.

- Color: The blanket is blue and all the stars are white.
- Numbers: There are groups of stars and single stars.
- Shape: The shapes of the stars are all the same.
- Size: The stars are different sizes.
- Space: There are larger areas of blue spaces between white stars.
- Texture: The blanket and stars are soft and fuzzy.

Parent-Baby Explorations

Patiently observe your baby's expressive responses in play. She may be developing her body awareness or practicing a new movement like rolling over to side lying. When your baby is quietly focused on her body movement and play explorations, observe what she is doing.

Parent-baby exploration 1

If your baby is not rolling to a side-lying position, place a primary colored or favorite toy that will motivate your baby:

- To roll onto the right side of her body.
- To roll onto the left side of her body.

Parent-baby exploration 2

When your baby is rolling over onto one side:

- Hold a brightly colored toy to encourage your baby's downward visual gaze and head flexion.

- Encourage the movement on both sides of his body.

Parent-baby exploration 3

Eye-hand coordination and everything your baby touches expands your baby's tactile sense and experiential learning.

- Introduce your baby to a variety of age-appropriate toys for mouthing and handling skills in play.

Self-Motivated Learning in the Prone Position

Rolling Over to Get Her Doll

Elle is lying on top of her favorite small fabric doll, and this motivates her to roll over so she can get it. Babies are beginning to separate both their arms and both their legs from each other. Let's look at her abilities and watch how she moves to get what she wants.

Elle reaches across her body with her left arm, and with increased hip mobility she can flex her left leg higher, moving her pelvis over her extended leg in a gradated movement onto her tummy. The weight-bearing side of her body provides support for the movement.

Over and Under

Lying on her back Elle feels her doll under her right shoulder. Rolling over, Elle problem solves how to release and grasp her doll.

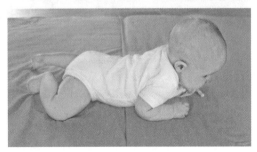

Spatial Awareness

With bright eyes Elle shares her pleasure in successfully releasing the doll from under her body and grasping it in her left hand. In the prone position, she brings the doll between her hands so that she is now above her doll. Elle is learning the spatial concept of over and under.

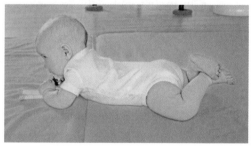

Tummy-Time Play with a Doll

Supported on her forearms in the prone position, tummy time is beginning to be a functional play position for four-month-old babies. With her doll near enough to reach, Elle grasps it with both hands.

Decision Making in Babies

Attention and Focus

Curiosity motivates the baby to move and play. Babies are dynamic explorers and reaching a desired toy can present new movement challenges. Age-appropriate activities provide dynamic experiences that encourage a baby's problem-solving skills.

In self-motivated play, babies focus and organize their actions to contact objects within reach. Visual processing and concentrated attention develops when babies discover a variety of ways to explore a toy or object. The little doll Elle is playing with is upside down, and she feels the wooly yarn hair with the palm of her hand. Through their handling skills babies learn about special properties of toys: shape, size, weight, softness, and texture.

Elle pushes the doll away and watches what happens. The doll turns over and her legs fly up in the air.

And then the doll's legs fall down on the mat. Elle reaches for her doll with open hands.

As they expand their visual attention, four-month-old babies perceive specific properties of the toy or object they are handling. They also explore new eye-hand coordination abilities.

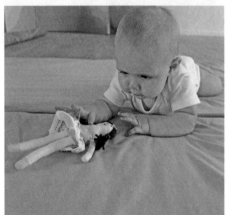

Indirect Focus

Elle focuses on the sensory stimulation she experiences by mouthing her hand and the fabric of the doll's skirt. Mouthing toys provides the baby's lips and tongue with abundant tactile stimulation and information about texture.

Goal-Directed Actions and Gestures **83**

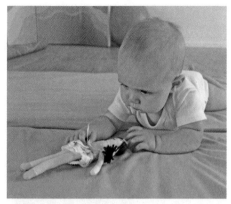

Direct Focus

Supported on her forearms, it's the little shiny pink ribbon that captures Elle's attention. Grasping the little ribbon she increases pressure between her thumb and index finger developing her fine motor skills.

Bright Eyes and Little Smiles

When parents are on the floor at their baby's level, they may notice their baby smiling with pleasure at what she can do. Holding the ribbon in one hand and grasping the doll's legs in her other hand, Elle looks up and shares her pleasure and mastery with bright eyes and a little smile.

A Little Orange Bead

Elle is now playing with her toy rattle that has colored beads and two large disks on a spiral wire. She coordinates her hands to first separate the orange bead from the green one, and then she touches the orange bead with her left index finger.

Next Elle grasps the small orange bead between her right index and middle finger. Pausing, she holds onto the bead and looks at it. We notice Elle's lateral weight-shift onto one forearm that occurs with her visual focus and head rotation.

Elle can separate the bead she wants from the green bead next to it. The beads are all hard but have different shapes, colors, and sizes. Mouthing the toy after handling it provides Elle with new information about what she sees and what she senses with her mouth and hands.

A Yellow Bead with a Smiley Face

Elle grasps the large red disk with her left hand and continues mouthing and grasping the thin wire while playing with her toy rattle.

The little yellow bead with a smiley face captures Elle's attention. She opens and spreads her left hand on top of the red disk. Supported on her forearms, Elle isolates and extends her index finger to point and touch the familiar smiley face she recognizes on the bead. Her little fingers of both hands maintain contact with the mat, and this contact stabilizes the large red disk and small yellow bead.

Shadows, Shapes, and Spirals

Elle now focuses on the large blue block, and she spreads her fingers to grasp the block with her whole hand. She grasps the block between her thumb on one side and her little finger on the other side, learning about the size, shape, and contour of the block.

The light is changing in the room, and Elle's fingers cast interesting shadows on the face of the block, and her fingers' shapes attract her attention.

See the Shadows

There is a yellow dotted spiral painted on the face of the blue block, but it is the shadows and shapes of her fingers moving that capture her interest.

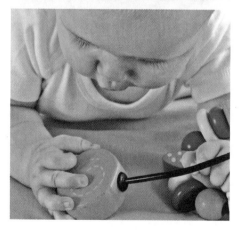

One Finger at a Time

Focused on her hand, Elle isolates and curls her index finger. She will eventually learn to isolate and move each finger individually. As she does this, she notices the shapes of the shadows.

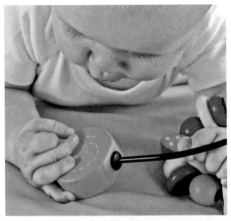

Thumb to Middle Finger

Her little finger stays in contact with the mat stabilizing the block. This allows Elle to maintain control while she brings her thumb and middle finger together to touch each other.

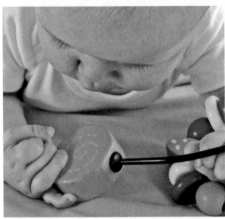

The Fourth Finger

Elle intensifies her grip as she observes the fourth finger's shadow getting longer and larger. The shadows of her other fingers show a decreasing contrast.

Mouthing the Block

Elle opens her hand to hold the flat surface and edge of the round block; then she lowers her head to mouth the block.

She isolates her index finger to bring her thumb and middle finger together. Beginning at this early stage, this manual ability will be used in everyday functional activities such as holding a spoon to feed herself, coloring with a crayon, and later in more complex activities such as playing a musical instrument.

In each of these vignettes, first playing with her doll and a longer exploration with the toy rattle, a four-month-old baby expands her potential for discovery play with each complex handling exploration.

These toy explorations followed one after the other during a forty-five minute play session. Let's review her movement and actions:

- Elle is lying in the prone position and weight-bearing on both forearms.
- She uses bilateral symmetrical hand movements to explore toys.
- She can weight-shift to the side but can't support herself on one arm yet.
- She can tuck her chin to look down at her hands.
- She can mouth the toy on the floor but can't yet bring the toy up to her mouth.

Expanding her focus of attention and visual abilities in guiding her movement explorations with toys and objects, Elle develops her manual dexterity and fine motor skills.

Observing Elle's goal-directed actions in these vignettes, we learn that:

- Elle focuses on the color and shape of the little orange bead and problem solves how to grasp the bead.
- She recognizes the familiar smiley face on her own toy rattle, and isolates and extends her right index finger to point to it.
- She shifts her focus of attention as she watches the shadows changing shape with the movement of her fingers.
- She isolates and curls her index finger to bring her other fingers together to touch each other.
- She can extend all her fingers and also curl all her fingers together.
- She can isolate her index finger and her other fingers depending on the action.
- She is learning about size, shape, and moving shadows.
- She smiles at the familiar, friendly smiley face on the bead.

As we follow the baby's natural movement development, we look at the baby's posture in the supine and prone positions. The baby's postural position and movement development are essential to the baby's expressive communication, exploration of toys and objects, and actions in the environment. During this month, in the supine position, a baby can easily communicate using the pointing gesture. Also from the supine position a baby can follow her index finger to roll over onto her front in the prone position. Babies demonstrate their competence when taking the lead to engage a parent or adult in their social interactions. In this month, we show how a baby uses the pointing gesture to direct an adult's attention to look at the stars on her favorite blanket.

Observing and responding to a baby's preverbal communication cues expand our social interaction repertoire with babies. When a baby directs an adult's attention by pointing to an object, *and* the adult responds to the baby's intention, the baby feels understood. Recognizing

the baby's goal to share her everyday experiences in looking and touching the stars on her blanket, confirms the baby's success in communicating.

When a baby orchestrates a complex action plan she learns to focus and follow through in a sequence of movements: first lying on her back, exploring a toy in side lying, and then rolling over onto her front in the prone position to experience her environment from a new perspective.

In the prone position new symmetrical-movement patterns contribute to a baby's bimanual explorations. Manual explorations in fingering toys and objects lead to new information processing, advancing the baby's social and cognitive development.

Four Month Chapter Review

• • • • •

DEVELOPMENTAL MOVEMENT

- Body awareness: Babies are developing the typical hands-on-knees contact in the supine position and hand-to-hand explorations in the prone position.
- Spinal-movement patterns: Your baby's shapely cervical curve is visible.
- Rolling over: Your baby rolls over from the supine to the prone position.
- Symmetrical-movement patterns: Symmetrical patterns include movement of both arms and/or both legs together.
- Visual processing: Looking down at their hands in the prone position indicates a baby's visual system is maturing.
- Lateral weight-shifting: Weight-shifts to each side prepare a baby to free one arm for reaching.

SOCIAL INTERACTION

- Active engagement: Babies take the lead in their social interactions.
- Pointing gestures: In the supine position a baby can use the pointing gesture to communicate.
- Expressive communication: Babies smile more, begin babbling, and coo with more sounds.

Four Month Chapter Review (cont.)

● ● ● ● ●

SELF-MOTIVATED LEARNING

- Pleasure in play: Uninterrupted play develops concentration so babies complete their activities at their own pace, taking pleasure in discovery play.
- Actions: Goal-directed action plans on the floor generate new experiences and learning.
- Symmetrical patterns: The symmetrical patterns contribute to bimanual explorations and fingering toys and objects.
- Motivation to mastery: Babies act on their own curiosity and regulate their motivation to problem solve.
- Over-and-under concept: Babies roll over onto a toy and problem solve how to retrieve it.

Month Five

●　●　●　●　●

Intention in Social Interactions and Actions

Your five-month-old baby builds on the essential movement abilities he developed at four months. These developmental movements in the prone position are based on symmetrical movement, midline orientation, and coordination of both hands to carry out his visual-manual explorations.

Five-month-old babies explore new movements in a variety of positions, with some key developments beginning this month. If you belong to a parenting group, you may see some babies lying on their back holding onto their feet or rolling over onto the front of their body in the prone position, while other babies will be practicing their reaching skills. You may notice your baby lying on her side to look at you or play with a toy.

In the supine position, babies continue to develop their body awareness and visual-tracking skills. Through their mouthing activity babies explore their body and the environment and expand their manual dexterity skills with toys and objects.

Two new movement patterns emerge that contribute to the development of your baby's body image. These are the symmetrical-push and lateral-push patterns. In tummy-time play five-month-old babies can practice a variety of weight-shift patterns. Weight-bearing on one arm frees the other arm for reaching and increased articulation. Playing in the side-lying position offers new possibilities for movement and exploration.

You will enjoy lots of family fun in your playful interactions on the floor this month. Babies are developing a sense of humor and can now take the lead in more complex, sophisticated social interactions. They improvise new responses, often accompanied by lots of chuckles and laughter, and they will take the initiative to keep the game going.

★ Developmental Movement

Body Awareness: In the Supine Position

Because of their ability to control their movements, babies can now grasp their feet, without rolling over, and reach across the midline of their body.

Hands to Feet and Feet to Mouth

Active hip flexion and extension have increased so the baby is able to raise her pelvis up off the floor.

Here, Elle holds her right foot in her right hand and grasps her toes with her mouth.

Movement and Visual Processing

Elle raises her left leg higher and looks at her foot as it comes into her visual field.

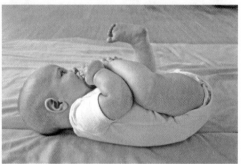

Elle lowers her left leg with more anti-gravity control.

Matching Heels and Symmetry

Symmetry is based on the body's midline and vertical axis. Differentiating both sides of the body develops in all positions: lying on the back, lying on the front, and, as you will observe this month, in side lying.

Turning her head to look at her toes, Elle reaches across her body with her right hand as if to grasp her left foot.

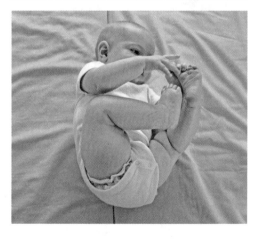

Matching Heel to Heel

But then she raises her right foot higher and grasps the toes of her right foot with her right hand.

Elle is holding her left foot in her left hand and grasps her right foot with her right hand, so she is holding onto each foot. Elle aligns her feet and brings both her heels together to touch each other at her midline.

Symmetrical and Lateral Patterns

Notice Elle's head-to-tail spinal alignment. Without looking at her feet, she holds her feet with her hands at her body's midline. Elle then releases her right hand and lets go of her right foot.

Body-Half Pattern

Maintaining her head in midline in this body-half exploration, Elle continues holding onto the toes of her left foot with her fingers of her left hand. She then extends both her left arm and leg, opening her limbs to her left side. In this bilateral movement she is differentiating each side of her body, one from the other in this body-half pattern.

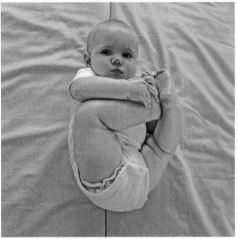

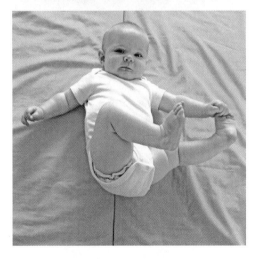

Visual Circular Tracking: Half Circle

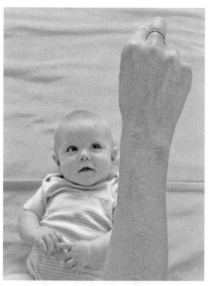

With improved horizontal, vertical, and diagonal tracking, babies now begin circular tracking of a toy or object when lying on their back. By four months babies begin to use their eyes independently, with less head movement.

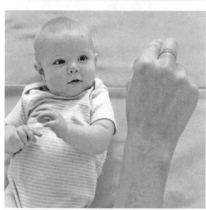

In this tracking sequence, we notice that Elle can visually coordinate both eyes together to track a set of keys in a circular direction on her left side. Elle's mother has the keys in her right hand and as she moves her hand in a half circle, she sings a little nursery rhyme.

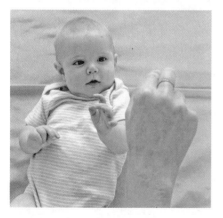

Round and round the mulberry bush. The monkey chased the weasel.

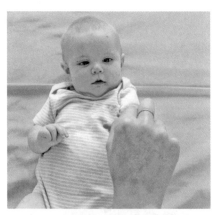

The monkey stopped to pull up his socks, POP! goes the weasel.

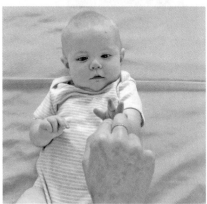

Elle's hands expressively respond in this little nursery-rhyme game. Her vision directs her reach for the keys.

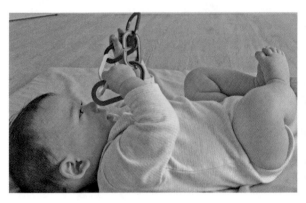

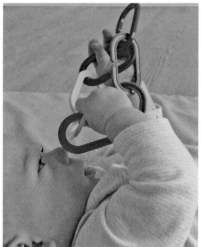

Tomas and a Chain of Colored Links

Eye-Hand Coordination

Tomas sees a chain of colored links on the mat and is ready to play. He grasps the chain of links between his hands. He handles and manipulates this new toy to explore what he can do.
He focuses on the blue link in his left hand. Then he focuses on the red link in his right hand.

Two Blue Links

Tomas holds a yellow link in each hand and raises the chain up to discover there are two blue links between them.

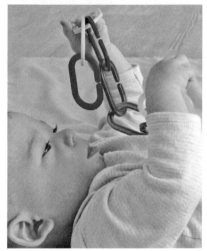

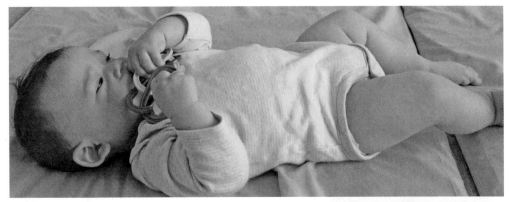

Tomas Grasps Two Blue Links

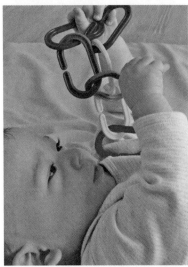

Mouthing Toys

Tomas brings the chain of links to his mouth. Mouthing his hand while holding the yellow links in both hands, he raises the chain above his head and releases the yellow link. Now he has both blue links in his left hand.

How did Tomas do this? In a show of manual dexterity, he slides his thumb through the center of one blue link to hold onto it and clasps the other link with his fourth and fifth fingers.

Next, Tomas has one blue link in his left hand and the second blue link in his right hand. What does this tell us?

Exploring this new toy for the first time, Tomas is rapidly developing his eye-hand coordination by grasping, handling, and mouthing. He manipulates the chain of links to grasp the color he wants in each hand.

All the links are all the same shape, but they are different colors: red, green, yellow, and blue.

Manual Dexterity and Making Connections

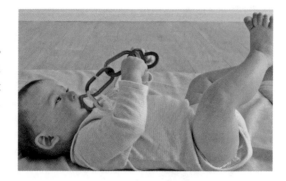

This fifteen-minute play session with a toy that Tomas explored for the first time raises some important developmental questions to consider:

Manual Dexterity

- What is Tomas discovering?
- What grasping and handling skills does he use?
- What does he learn by mouthing the links?
- What does alternating his leg position between raising and lowering his legs tell us?

Making Connections

- All the links are the same shape.
- All the links are the same size.
- The links are different colors.
- Mouthing toys informs him about size, shape, texture, and hardness.
- He uses vision and mouthing to grasp and manipulate the toy to separate one colored link from another.
- He can move his legs in symmetrical flexion, extension, and mid-range movements.

Symmetrical-Movement Patterns

Babies initiate the symmetrical patterns by pushing with both hands and/or both feet together. These patterns help your baby to differentiate and integrate his upper body from his lower body. Four-month-old babies support themselves on their forearms in the prone position. Five-month-old babies can push with both hands and extend their elbows.

Weight-Shift

During tummy-time play, babies practice a variety of weight-shift patterns. Symmetrical-movement patterns provide stability as Elle pushes with both her feet. Directing her visual focus upward she shifts her weight onto her left arm to look at the doll her mother is playfully showing her.

Lateral-Movement Patterns

Babies initiate the lateral patterns with a push of their hand and/or push of their foot on the same side of their body. These patterns help your baby differentiate and integrate each side of his body.

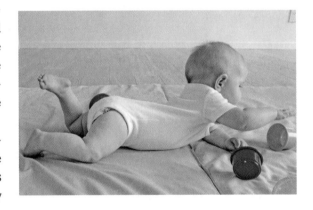

With more control in a lateral weight-shift to the side, one side of the baby's body elongates while the other side of his body flexes.

Moving to reach a toy, this baby initiates the movement sequence with a push of the right foot that elongates the same side of the body in reaching forward with his right hand. The left side of his body is supporting, freeing the right side of his body to move and develop his reaching skills.

Spinal-Movement Patterns

The side-lying position is a more dynamic position for play. With more options, babies explore new coordinated movements between their arms and legs. Separating arms from each other, and legs from each other, and positioning one foot in front for stability, Elle challenges her dynamic balance. She explores maintaining toe contact with the mat and reaching behind with her free arm before she loses balance to roll backward or return to the side-lying position. Separating arms and legs from each other is a precursor of belly crawling, hands-and-knees creeping, and walking.

Spinal Rotation

In the side-lying position, five-month-old babies can lift their head, flex their body (spinal lateral flexion), and rotate their head and chest to look behind them.

Movement Patterns in Play—Pivoting

In the prone position, your baby may begin to move her arms and legs independently, differentiating her arms from each other and her legs from each other. Babies begin pivoting between five and six months. Pivoting in the prone position provides babies with a new ability to shift their weight on extended arms. Babies can now develop new action plans to obtain a toy by reaching out to the same side of their body without rolling over.

Pivoting in a Half Circle

Elle performs two different actions with her arms. She pushes with her left hand and extends her elbow. She supports herself on her hand while she reaches out to the right side with her arm. Both legs are also performing different actions; one leg flexes and her other leg extends.

She lifts her left arm and shifts her weight and reaching with her left arm she elongates the left side of her body. She alternates her arms to reach, support, and pivot.

In between pivoting actions, Elle flexes both her legs and momentarily brings her feet together at her midline.

If Elle continues reaching to her right side with her toy, she will eventually pivot in a full circle.

Movement with a Toy Parrot

With both arms flexed, Elle supports herself by weight-bearing on both forearms and looks down at her little toy parrot. What can we tell about Elle's movement development by observing her holding the toy parrot with both hands at her midline?

With both arms flexed she supports herself on her forearms. The lower limbs are becoming more active. Hip extension increases and she is able to flex and lift both her legs off the mat against gravity.

Next she rests both her legs on the floor. She places one hand on top of the other and looks down at the toy parrot between her hands.

The spinal-movement patterns establish the babies' head-to-tail connection, providing the internal core support to coordinate their arms and legs in relationship to each other and to their whole body. With improved head control Elle looks down at the top of the parrot's head. Demonstrating antigravity control of her legs, she lifts her forelegs off the mat and brings her feet together.

Flinging a Toy Parrot on a Yellow Ring

This month babies can shift their weight to each side and support themselves on one forearm. This frees the opposite arm for reaching, which lets Elle explore flexing and extending her arm in space. In this sequence we notice the toy has two rings: one large yellow ring that the parrot slides on and a smaller green ring.

Supporting herself on her forearms, Elle grasps the large yellow ring, flinging and flapping the lightweight toy parrot around. Let's look at the spatial directions of her movements:

Reaching sideways

Supported on her right forearm, Elle lifts and waves the parrot by extending her left arm and reaching out to the side.

Without looking and with her arm still off the mat, she flexes her elbow.

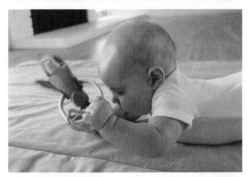

Reaching forward

With her arm still in the air, she extends her arm and reaches forward. When the parrot gets too close, she protects herself by fluttering and closing her eyes.

On both forearms

She flexes her elbow and brings her left arm back onto the floor. Looking at her parrot, Elle integrates her exhilarating experience.

Hand to mouth to hand

Holding the larger yellow ring in her hand, Elle releases her grip and transfers the toy from her left hand to her mouth and then to her right hand.

Hand-to-hand and hand-to-mouth-to-hand transfers occur more frequently when babies lie on their front in tummy-time play and support themselves on both forearms.

Elle pauses after her play session. Her experiences handling the crinkly toy parrot and mouthing the yellow ring provides Elle with abundant auditory, visual, tactile, and kinesthetic stimulation.

Bimanual Play with a Toy Plane

A baby may use her preferred hand in a more active role, as in this exploration, to grasp and turn the wheel of a plane, while the opposite hand holds the plane to keep it steady.

Elle approaches the wheel of the plane with an open hand and then lowers her hands onto the mat. Looking down at her hands she brings them together, matching and touching her thumbs and fingers to each other.

She approaches the plane to grasp the wheel and refines her grasp by using the precision side of her hand.

This five-month-old manipulates the wheel of her toy plane using a precision grasp with her thumb and index finger. Her opposite hand takes on a supporting role by stabilizing the plane.

Five-month-old babies can handle objects in increasingly complex ways. With concentrated attention, Elle coordinates her hand actions, using both hands to play with and explore the wheel of her plane. She actively grips the wheel with one hand, while her opposite hand touches the edge of the wheel with her index finger. Both index fingers are holding the rim of the grey wheel.

Elle is able to turn the wheels and the propeller of the plane. However she can't turn the wheel around continuously using only her index finger (as a ten-month-old baby could).

In these longer play sequences we see Elle's increased ability to regulate her attention and focus on this toy that offers new possibilities for her discriminating hand actions. We observe closely to see how she uses the precision side of the hand for active bimanual exploration.

Her interest in her toy plane is that her mother is a pilot, so Elle is familiar with planes and flying, which provides an added incentive to her exploration.

Side-Lying Position for Dynamic Play

Spinal Patterns

The spinal-movement patterns establish the baby's head-to-tail connection in all three positions:

- Extension lying on the front
- Flexion lying on the back
- Lateral flexion in side lying

Side-Lying Position

A significant development occurs this month when your baby rolls over to maintain a new side-lying position for play. In side lying, the supporting side of her body is extended and the opposite side is laterally flexed. You may have noticed this lateral flexion when your baby rolls over. From this position, if a baby hears a sound or you call her name from behind, she can rotate her body to turn and look behind. This means your baby now has full range of control of her head.

Extending One Arm Overhead

Playing in this new side-lying position, babies can hold a lightweight toy in one hand. Some babies will play with their head resting on the floor, but if the toy is light enough a baby can lift her head up off the floor and support her body on her forearm. Elle's lightweight ball has holes large enough to grasp with her fingers and hold in one hand. Extending her arm she waves the ball overhead. When she looks up to track the toy, she is developing her visual-movement skills.

Rolling from Side Lying to Supine

Elle is playing in the side-lying position; Elle supports herself on one forearm and extends her leg on the same side of the body. Crossing her right leg over her left, she flexes her head and looks downward while positioning her foot for support and stability. To maintain her balance in this position she extends her arm outward on the same side of her body.

Elle challenges her balance and explores reaching backward with her extended arm; this initiates the movement for rolling from her side onto her back.

Elle begins rolling, releasing both legs from the supporting surface. She maintains control of her head with finely tuned head flexion and lateral head righting (holding her head up off the floor). Through this finely gradated series of movements, Elle rolls over onto her back.

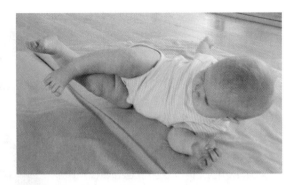

Now that Elle has experienced rolling over from her side onto her back, she will go on to master this movement during the next month.

Note: Provide a safe space on a play-mat or carpet for babies to explore rolling over without hurting themselves.

When your baby rolls over from the prone position to play in side lying, her sensory experience activates many body systems:

- The visual system gives her a new perspective of her surroundings.
- The vestibular system contributes to the awareness of where she is in space.
- The kinesthetic system informs her of her body and limb position, and their state of activity or rest.
- The haptic system includes tactile pressure inputs that contribute to shaping the ribcage.

The dynamic action of rolling over onto both sides of the body provides a baby with all these important developmental benefits.

♥ Social Interaction

Spatial Alignment in Social Play

From the beginning babies are aware when the parent or an adult they are interacting with is engaged and interested in what they are doing. In this section on spatial interactions, you will learn how to position your body to enhance your playtime with your baby. Babies build on the social skills they learn through play and are motivated to improvise new ways to keep a parent or caregiver engaged.

Spatial awareness occurs naturally as babies develop their body awareness, body image, and body position in relationship to others, and to objects in their environment. Through social play, babies embody the concepts of direction, dimension, distance, and location, which develop their overall spatial awareness.

Partners in Play

This parent and baby engage by smiling, touching, and vocalizing. Horizontal alignment encourages a variety of ways to interact together. Lying beside your baby, she can widen her arm to roll over and touch you. You can also scoop your baby up into your arms and roll your baby on top of your body. Improvising in play together, you can enclose each other in an embracing hug.

Parallel Play

This family enjoys participating in a new movement session at their baby's level, lying on the floor, shoulder-to-shoulder, in the prone position. This vertical alignment also encourages the baby's parallel play with his older brother nearby.

Interactive Play

Face-to-face body positioning in sagittal alignment encourages hand-to-hand contact when you and your baby are in close proximity to each other. Expanding the space between the two of you can change the activity into a two-way, back-and-forth ball game. Through interactive games, babies develop an understanding of near and far and the distance of the ball rolling across the space between you.

Movement is Functional and Expressive

Movement is both functional and expressive. In everyday situations both of these aspects are integrated naturally into your baby's movement repertoire. Functional movements are based on the baby's movement development and manual skills. You can observe the functional aspect of movement in the way your baby performs a desired action: for example, when your baby pushes or sweeps a toy out of the way. At the same time, if he turns his head away he is expressively letting you know he is ready for a change of scenery or new activity. Or when your baby begins feeding himself and pushes a dish of peas away with tightly pursed lips, you know exactly how he feels.

Mutual Playfulness

What is amazing when interacting with a baby is that we don't know what will happen next. How will your baby complete a sequence in play? Who will take the next turn when you and your baby are engaged in social interaction? In this early preverbal stage many unexpected actions and interactions spontaneously occur that will surprise and delight you.

Expressive Communication

Interacting with your baby at his level on the floor enhances your relationship because you experience the environment from your baby's perspective. As you engage in more complex social interactions, you, your family, and caregivers will

engage your baby in more expressive dialogues. Spontaneous, playful actions between a baby and parent can start with smiling that sparks a new social interaction.

Postures, Gestures, and Whole Body Actions

To understand the meaning of movement we also observe the baby's expressive postures and gestures in social interactions.

Postures

A posture is a movement that is consistent through the whole body. The five-month-old baby's lateral body position supports her expressive communication. She can shift her weight to support herself on each side of her body to reach and gesture with her opposite hand.

Gestures

A gesture is an isolated movement expressed in one or more individual parts of the body. Lying in the prone position, Elle gestures by isolating and pointing her index finger.

Communication and Whole Body Actions

Whenever communication is accompanied by integrated whole body actions in adults we perceive their expression to be genuine. Recognizing your baby's postures and gestures is fundamental for understanding his functional and expressive movement communication.

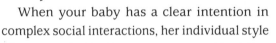

When your baby has a clear intention in complex social interactions, her individual style of communicating becomes more evident through her whole-body actions.

A Baby's Playful Surprise

Intention in Social Interactions

The following social interaction demonstrates the baby's intention to interact with an adult who is engaged in what she is doing. The baby is not imitating the adult's actions, and the adult pauses and waits for the baby's response to see what she will do next. As you read this vignette, observe what engages the baby's curiosity and interest to stimulate her to lead the next interaction. We can see the baby's initiative to keep the game going as she continues to add a new focus of attention, and then we see her take the initiative to end the game in a surprising action.

Floor Moves: Face to face

In this engaging interaction, Kaya is lying on the floor in the prone position. She can support herself by weight-bearing on her forearms and can shift her weight to each side. Kaya is able to perform separate actions with her arms and hands; she can reach forward, and she can cross her midline with her hand. All these actions tell us she is a developing five-month-old. I am lying on the floor in the prone position supported on both forearms facing Kaya.

Five-month-old babies lying on their front can shift their weight to each side, freeing one arm for expressive play. In the prone position and in close contact with a social partner, this baby finds new ways to interact using her new reaching skills.

Focus of Attention

Facing me in the prone position on the floor—Kaya tucks her chin that enhances her downward visual gaze. Her focus of attention is centered between my hands. In our close proximity, she begins touching the little finger of my right hand with the fingers of her left hand, mirroring the same side of my body.

Matching Fingers

Making hand-to-hand contact, Kaya rotates her head to her left side, looking down at our hands. Kaya matches and touches three fingers on my right hand with the same three fingers of her left hand.

Shift of Attention

Kaya maintains hand contact, with her left hand on top of my right hand. Her focus shifts as she is attracted by the motion and sparkling color of my necklace.

Notice Kaya's head-to-tail alignment and the shapely neck curve she's developing through her tummy-time play. Because five-month-old babies can shift their weight to each side and free one hand for reaching, they can perform separate actions with each hand. Increasing pressure with her left hand on top of my right hand, Kaya extends her left elbow and also maintains support with her softly flexed right hand.

Active Engagement

Kaya begins a sequence of engaged interactions.

She looks up and notices I am smiling at her. My expressive response lets her know that I'm enjoying her touch and I am interested in what she's doing in our playtime together.

We interact by gazing at each other in this mutual, moment-to-moment interaction.

Smiling Together

Next Kaya smiles at me. We are totally engaged in our playful time together, and we smile at each other to express our mutual pleasure in this nonverbal social interaction. Kaya maintains her hand-to-hand contact, with both hands softly open.

As Kaya and I continue playing together, we are sharing in a moment-to-moment dynamic interaction. I can't anticipate what Kaya will do next, which is where the element of surprise in her game comes in. By smiling I am letting Kaya know that I am enjoying and interested in what she is doing. This is what gives her the freedom to spontaneously change the game and interaction in her own way.

Intention in Interaction

Kaya is a playful partner in our spontaneous play session. As the game develops she is motivated to continue taking the lead in the next action. Watching me closely Kaya maintains her focus on my face and, at the same time, shifts her weight onto her supporting right arm. Kaya initiates a new reaching action forward and across to touch my opposite hand.

A Baby's Playful Surprising Action: Timing in Interaction

Maintaining eye contact in this integrated response, Kaya suddenly pulls her hand away and simultaneously opens her mouth and eyes wide. She flexes her left arm and extends both legs in the air, with her right hand lightly touching the floor. Her accelerated, spontaneous response adds an element of playful surprise. Kaya expressively ends the game and laughs at her playful action! She decides when to pull her hand away with a surprisingly quick action that she finds funny. Laughing, she looks at me to see if I find it funny too!

Making Us Smile

Vasudevi Reddy, professor of developmental and cultural psychology at the University of Portsmouth, writes that far from being constrained by their lack of speech, infants do intentional actions in a social context to make others smile or laugh by playing "jokes" through their expressive movement, quick actions, and vocalizations.[1]

What is it that Kaya does in this game that makes it so funny? There is a beginning, middle, and end in this social interaction: In face-to-face alignment on the floor we begin with her interest and focus of attention; in the middle, we are engaged and smiling together and Kaya keeps the game going with each new action. Then, she suddenly pulls her hand away and ends our playtime with this surprising action.

Kaya doesn't have to plan her actions. She spontaneously and playfully interacts with a partner she knows well. She takes the lead with each action. Kaya skillfully directs a surprise ending that she finds funny, looking at me to see if I find it funny too.

Developmental Abilities Enhance Play

At five months Kaya demonstrates the following:

- She has good head control in the prone position.
- She supports herself weight-bearing on her forearms.
- She shifts her weight to both sides.
- She reaches across her midline to interact.
- She pulls her hand away from the floor using accelerated timing.

Parent-Baby Explorations: On the Floor

Face-to-face: in the prone position

- Lie down on a mat, or a carpeted or wood floor.
- Lie face-to-face to encourage communication.
- Support yourself on your forearms.
- Let your baby take the lead.

Interaction

- Touch your baby's hand on the side that mirrors the same side of your body; for example, the fingers of your right hand touch the fingers of your baby's left hand.
- Pause and quietly observe your baby's response.

Expressive communication cues

- Smile at your baby to let her know you are enjoying her touch.
- Touch your baby's hand and pause to observe what your baby will do next.
- Touch both your baby's hands and slide your hands back.
- Pause to let your baby take the lead and delight in what she does.

Partners in Play

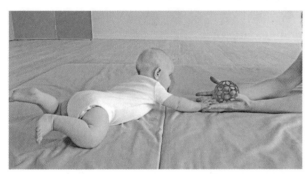

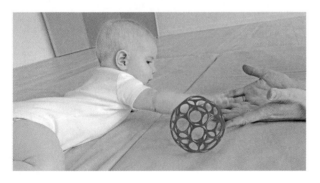

A First Ball Game

In this ball game between a parent and baby, they both focus their eyes and direct their hands to roll or to catch the ball. Parent and baby interact as partners in the ball play game, sharing taking the lead.

Elle can grasp and hold this lightweight ball easily in her hand.

Her mother places her arms with open hands on the mat. Anticipating the action, Elle gets the idea that her mother wants her to give her the ball.

Her mother extends her arms and hands. Because the ball rolls easily, Elle can roll it or place it in her mother's hands.

Playing ball provides a context for social interaction. Elle reaches, touches, and holds onto her mother's hand, playing with her fingers.

Mouthing the Ball

After the ball game with her mother, Elle mouths the ball. Mouthing and exploring toys with their tongue provide babies with abundant oral stimulation. Moving her tongue in and out of her mouth, Elle playfully explores the ball. She looks down to watch her tongue as she slides it in and out of the ball's open shaped spaces.

● Self-Motivated Learning

A Yellow Duck Vignette: Solving an Upside-Down Puzzle

Babies learn to anticipate weight-shifting and automatically make postural adjustments prior to reaching for objects. Reaching, grasping, and handling toys and objects require new timing strategies to perform their goal-directed actions.

A new toy on the floor leads a baby to explore a sequence of movements and on-the-spot actions to reach her goal. When babies develop a course of action, they discover new solutions in play, and these action outcomes promote more advanced functioning at each stage of development.

Reaching

Elle's toy duck has rolled away from her and landed upside down. By supporting herself on one side of her body, Elle can shift her weight to free her opposite hand for reaching. Using a visually directed reach, she grasps her toy.

Mouthing the Bottom of the Toy

Elle grasps the toy duck with one hand and lifts the lightweight toy up off the mat. Supporting herself on her elbow, she rotates her right forearm so she can mouth the bottom of the toy.

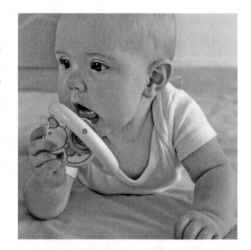

Both mouthing and handling a toy provides babies with information about size, shape, and hardness of the toy.

Problem-Solving Skills

Supporting herself on her forearms provides stability and control for her handling skills. Elle suspends the duck upside down while balancing the wooden ring between both hands. Centering the toy duck between her hands, she rotates her forearms, positioning her arms with the palms of her hands facing each other. Elle articulates her thumb and fingers and holds the wooden ring with the duck suspended between her hands. She controls the action so the toy doesn't roll away as she problem solves how to get the little duck upright.

Turning the Duck Right-Side Up

Supported on one forearm Elle grasps the wooden ring with her other hand. Balancing the toy on the ring, she looks at the toy from the side. She controls the action with her right hand, holding the ring with three fingers. Three fingers of her left hand mirror the action. She tips the duck over and it lands right-side up close to her body.

The Feel of her Arm: Matching Curved Shapes

Turning the toy over Elle sees the bottom, the side, and the top of the toy and its three-dimensional shape. She focuses on the toy, stabilizing the ring with her right hand. Seeing the duck's bill she opens her mouth wide. Elle matches the round shape of the wooden ring, enclosing the ring in the curved shape of her left arm.

Shaping Her Thumb and Index Finger

With concentrated attention on the duck's bill and without looking at her hand, Elle brings the tip of her right thumb to her middle finger. Then she presses them together. At the same time she coordinates her left hand to stabilize the rocking ring. This prevents the duck from rolling forward on the two green wheels.

Grasping the Duck's Bill

Elle spreads her middle finger and thumb apart and matches her grasp to the small shape. The little-finger side of both her hands stabilizes the toy on the mat. Shaping her thumb and index finger, she uses a more precise grasp to grip the duck's bill.

Handling and Exploring Toys

In this vignette Elle is exploring the wooden duck for the very first time. By five months, babies have gained a variety of experiences exploring their hands and fingers and shaping their hands to objects. Handling and maneuvering toys with their hands provides babies with important tactile information and a three-dimensional experience of the toy's shape and size and enables them to explore a toy from a variety of visual perspectives.

Problem Solving to Stabilize the Toy Duck

Babies learn how to maintain their balance in dynamic interactions with gravity. They create action plans and problem solve how to explore a toy or object to reach their goal. If the toy is mobile, like this yellow duck on wheels, the baby has new challenges, such as figuring out how to stabilize the toy so she can grasp the part of the toy she is focusing on.

Releasing a Toy

Babies use a variety of hand actions to release a toy, transfer toys hand to hand, and grasp a specific part of the toy. Depending on the toy, a baby may use a pulling action to pull the toy out of one hand; or he can use momentum by holding onto the toy and sliding his hand back and forth on the floor to release a toy. Babies also use their mouth to discriminate specific parts of a toy and to transfer a toy from hand to mouth and mouth to hand.

Fine Motor Skills

Refining her grasp by shaping her thumb and index finger is an advanced grasping skill. Elle stabilizes the toy with the little-finger side of her left hand touching the toy and the mat. She regulates her attention by focusing on the duck's bill and successfully directs her thumb and index finger to grasp the bill, developing her fine motor skills.

Refinement of the precision side or skill side of the hand is achieved when the little-finger side stabilizes the activity.

Once Elle has successfully turned the toy duck upright, she repeats the action grasping the toy in a variety of ways.

Spatial Concept: Upside Down and Topside Up

How do babies recognize a toy is upside down? Once they explore turning the toy over, what else can they do? Will they repeat the action?

Exploring a toy provides a variety of challenges and stimulates babies to act in new ways that develop their fine motor skills.

Smiling and Pleasure in Play

What a delight to observe the baby's changing facial expressions as she plays with the toy duck. Her curiosity, her ability to focus, her skill in using her hands and fingers together, and her interest in what happens next motivate her to problem solve in a variety of ways.

The baby's expressive pleasure in discovering not just one solution—but a variety of solutions—builds the baby's self-confidence and competence.

Choreographing the Action

Let's look at this vignette from a different perspective. We know that babies are capable of acting in deliberate ways. We mentioned at the beginning of the book that babies develop their executive function in these early months. We can be more specific and outline the beginnings of this development.

In unstructured and uninterrupted play babies are free to move and follow their curiosity and interest in their play explorations. This baby focuses on the toy she is interested in.

Reaching for a toy may present a new situation; a baby can pause and develop a new course of action. This vignette shows a baby has a goal to reach a toy; she can adjust to a new situation and can regulate her motivation.

Next, a baby problem solves and develops an action plan to explore a toy. Because this baby is adaptable, she can adjust to the new situation and demonstrate her cognitive flexibility.

Through exploration babies learn three-dimensional information about toys and objects, and where a toy is located in the environment. In this vignette a baby explores the three-dimensional concept: upside down and topside up.

Self-produced movements, problem solving, and planning actions to reach their goal create the primary foundation on which babies build their success as self-motivated learners. Discovering new solutions in play, these action outcomes promote more advanced functioning.

Five Month Chapter Review

● ● ● ● ●

DEVELOPMENTAL MOVEMENT

- Lateral movement patterns: Lateral patterns include movement of the arm and leg together on the same side of the body.
- Body awareness: Babies bring hands to feet, and feet to mouth, and match feet heel to heel.
- Mouthing toys: Babies learn about taste, texture, hardness, and shapes.
- Rolling to side lying: Side lying activates many body systems: visual, vestibular, proprioceptive, and kinesthetic.
- Rolling to supine: From the side-lying position, babies roll onto their back and maintain lateral head righting by holding their head up off the floor.
- Pivoting in prone position: Babies begin to move their arms and legs independently.

SOCIAL INTERACTION

- Active engagement: An attentive parent waits to see what the baby will do next.
- Partners in play: Parent and baby connect though smiling, touching, and vocalizing.
- Spatial alignment: Parent and baby interact in new spatial alignments on the floor.
- Expressive communication: Situating yourself at the baby's level promotes back-and-forth interaction.

Five Month Chapter Review (cont.)

• • • • •

- Social skills: Babies develop social skills when they take the lead in a back-and-forth social game.
- Eye tracking: Babies can visually track a half circle to an action song.
- Timing: A baby can lead a social game by adding a surprising action that she finds funny.
- Pleasure in play: A baby's changing facial expressions show her pleasure during problem-solving explorations.

SELF-MOTIVATED LEARNING

- Mouthing: Babies mouth objects to gain information about the size, shape, and texture.
- Haptic sense: Babies can match the shape of their arm to a similar curved space of a toy.
- Grasping: Babies use more precise grasping patterns when the toy or objects have movable or small shapes.
- Upside-down concept: A baby recognizes a toy is upside down and problem solves how to stabilize and turn it topside up.
- Interactive ball game: Parent and baby focus on the ball as equals, providing the option for one or the other to take the lead.

Month Six

• • • • •

Exploring New Horizons

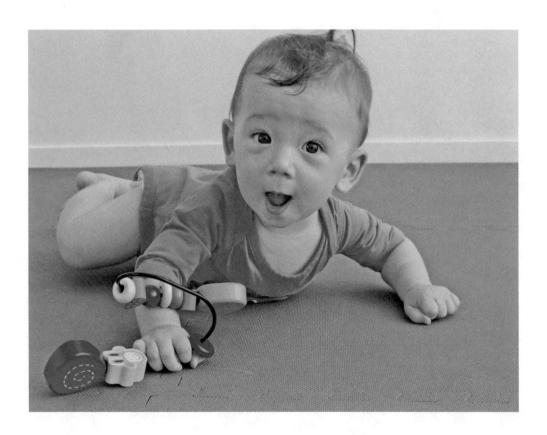

There is a great sense of anticipation this month now that your six-month-old baby is on the move. Increased balance of antigravity extensor and flexor control—in both supine and prone positions—enables babies to develop new locomotion patterns with more differentiated movements of their arms and legs. Babies push with both hands to extend their elbows and shift their weight, and in this more dynamic position they are beginning to reach forward and to the side to grasp a toy. When a baby pushes with her hands to extend her elbows and pushes with her toes to extend her knees, you may find her balancing in the push-up position.

Lying on the front of the body in the prone position is a more functional play position for your mobile baby this month. Exploring toys and the environment offer babies new problem-solving challenges in discovery play. Because you are tuned in to your baby's subtle communication cues, you patiently wait for your baby to invite you to play her game.

Space on the Floor to Move

Playing and moving on different floor surfaces provides a baby with new experiences. Carpeted floors are best for rolling; a wood floor is best to slide on (babies should not be placed on tile floors). Alternatively you can choose an interlocking play mat that is specifically designed for children of all ages.

With your baby's new interest in exploring the environment, parents and caregivers expand their active play at the baby's level on the floor. These floor activities reinforce the developmental movement patterns your baby is exploring and enhance your growing relationship.

★ Developmental Movement

Spinal Patterns

At four months your baby could lie on her tummy and extend her spine while supporting herself on her forearms. At five months she could extend her arms, one after the other, in a rocking motion on her belly. Now at six months she can fly like an airplane extending her whole body, with arms and legs reaching into space. Your baby continues to explore fully extending her spine to develop the muscles needed for rolling over, standing, and walking.

Fly Like an Airplane

This pivot-prone extension pattern is the opposite of the baby's whole body flexion pattern—the c-curve shape of the newborn.

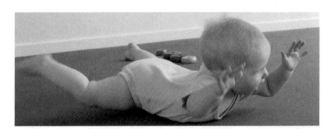

Rolling Over and Over

If the floor space is clear, some babies will roll over from supine to prone position and from prone to supine. Enjoying this activity a baby may continue rolling over and over, covering more space on the floor. Reaching the other side of the room, he may pause and begin rolling back to where he started from.

Symmetrical-Movement Patterns: Upper and Lower Body

For several months your baby has been diligently practicing and fine-tuning the symmetrical-movement patterns. At four months, she supported herself on her forearms, beginning to extend her elbows. The symmetrical patterns differentiate and integrate the upper and lower body and develop midline alignment. These symmetrical patterns are essential for your baby to develop integrated postures, binocular vision, and the ability to cross her body's midline.

Symmetrical Push from the Hands

Now, at six months babies are experimenting by lifting their body higher off the ground and pushing with both hands to move their body on the floor. Much to the baby's surprise however, she may find herself sliding backwards, farther away from the toy or person she was trying to reach.

On the floor, Sophera joyfully explores this new movement pattern. Babies develop muscle tone and strength by using both hands together to push their whole body against the resistance of gravity.

Spinal patterns support the symmetrical-push patterns. Sophera pushes with both hands to extend her arms. Arm extension is easier at six months than it was at five months.

Focusing on her hands Sophera is matching up her hands to each other; at the same time she flexes one leg. Babies with more postural control can flex one leg and extend the other; this movement prepares them for belly crawling.

Balancing in Push-ups

Like a gymnast your baby exercises both balance and control. She pushes up through her hands to extend her elbows and from her toes to extend her knees, lifting her whole body up off the floor to a higher-level pushup.

When balancing in this position, a baby may turn around to look at her feet. This expands her visual range and develops eye-foot coordination. Babies are learning to interact with the forces of weight, gravity, and balance in order to perform this dynamic action.

The push-up position is an example of yield-and-push patterns—patterns of *compression* that develop through one's relationship to *gravity*. In these patterns, babies yield to gravity and develop strength by pushing their whole body weight against the force of gravity.

Lateral-Movement Patterns: Right and Left Side

Lateral-movement patterns differentiate and integrate both sides of the body, and develop a lateral-line alignment. These patterns—initiated by the hand and/or foot on one side of the body—help your baby differentiate one side of the body from the other. When babies focus and reach forward into space with one hand, they develop the streamlined mobility and lightness in their body needed to explore larger areas in their environment.

Shifting Weight

With more control in a lateral weight-shift to the side, one side of the baby's body elongates while the other side flexes.

If you are on the floor with your six-month-old baby and call her name or make a sound, she may shift her weight to one side. This action causes her body to curve in an arc so that she can turn to look at you.

Lying on the Back: Supine Position

While lying on their back, babies still watch their hands-to-feet play closely and especially enjoy the tactile stimulation of mouthing their toes. Your baby's ability to reach across his body with both hands to play with one foot continues to develop an awareness of his body's midline. In diapering and body games your baby can flex and lift his head to watch you name the parts of his body he is exploring.

Tactile Stimulation

Six-month-old babies lying on their back can grasp a lightweight toy with one hand. The soft, fuzzy bear with contrasting hard discs stimulates a variety of tactile experiences.

Tomas is exploring the bear, and with one hand he discriminates between the soft fuzzy parts of the bear from the hard discs he touches with his other hand.

Mid-Range Position

Your baby demonstrates greater antigravity control this month. Tomas can symmetrically raise his feet off the floor, flex his knees, and hold this mid-range position comfortably without holding onto his legs.

In this mid-range position babies can flex their legs and reach with both hands to play with both feet. This play helps them develop their body awareness.

Extending Both Legs

Babies can also extend their legs vertically. In this position Sophera maintains some control with her arms flexed and hands closed, which prevents her legs from swaying too far sideways. At six months, balance reactions come into play in the supine position, and babies learn to adjust their body to prevent falling over to the side.

♥ Social Interaction

Up-and-Over Body Moves in Play

Before babies can crawl forward by alternating both sides of their body in the lateral pattern necessary for belly crawling, this curious six-month-old baby finds a new way to move her body forward in a playful body game with her mother.

Parents who are comfortable playing on the floor with their baby provide new ways for the baby to interact in the environment. The baby explores climbing onto her mother's legs but not all the way over onto the floor yet. This is the beginning of several climbing-up-and-over body games her mother will be improvising with her in the next few months.

With a push of her left foot, she reaches forward with her left hand, Elle explores one-half of this lateral movement pattern. Alternating sides is the beginning of a new belly crawling pattern she will add to her movement repertoire.

Pushing up Elle extends her elbows and supports herself on both hands. Although she wants to continue moving forward, she hasn't developed the full belly crawling pattern on the floor yet. By alternating sides the full lateral movement pattern opens up visual scanning. Visual scanning in the peripheral field is closely integrated with the baby's experience in belly crawling.

Playing with a Springy Orange Slinky

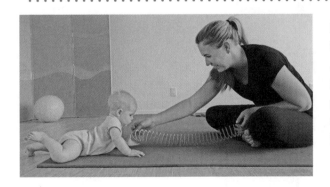

Elle has her eye on the colorful plastic, orange slinky toy. Although she can't reach it, her mother holds one end while giving Elle the other end, and she gently stretches the slinky between them.

Elle's mouth opens wide and her legs extend as she reaches forward for the toy.

What is surprising for Elle is what happens when she lets go and watches the slinky spring back to her mother, out of reach.

Her mother gives her the slinky, which now Elle can explore.

Wide and Narrow

With one finger on the rim, Elle presses the toy against the floor and pulls the end with her other hand to see what she can do.

She watches the spaces between the circular rings get wider and narrower.

Spontaneous Play: Improvising a Playful Hand Game

Elle and her mother engage in a hand-game interaction. Elle begins by looking intently at her mother's hands.

Her mother waits; Elle moves first and raises both her legs up off the floor in a beginning play move.

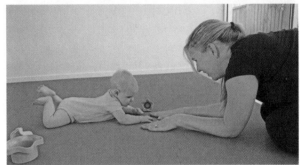

Her mother watches closely as Elle raises her right hand up off the floor continuing the game.

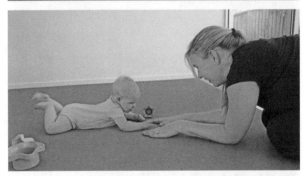

Her mother joins the game and raises both her hands off the floor as Elle watches closely. Her mother knows that Elle can do this movement.

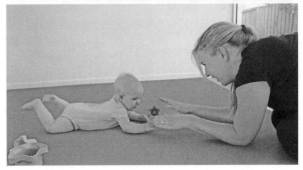

In concluding the sequence her mother turns her right hand over with her palm facing up, and Elle puts her right hand on top.

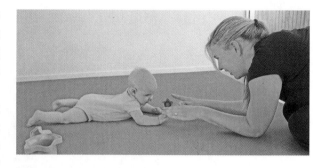

When playing together, wait for your baby to make the first move. Why not begin the game first? Because you don't know what your baby will do and you want to encourage her initiative.

By pausing and waiting, you are communicating a very important message to your baby. The meaning in your nonverbal message is that you are attentive and interested in what your baby is going to do and that you are playing this game *together*.

Elle's mother observes her baby closely. Elle makes the first two moves, and her mother waits to allow Elle enough time for her to make the next move, which she does. Last month, we observed a game where Kaya initiated similar actions with her partner in play and added an exhilarating ending to her game.

These exciting play sessions build your relationship with your baby; they develop focus, mutual attention, timing, spatial awareness, and social cooperation.

Reaching the Rainbow Tower

Attracted by a colorful stacking toy, Elle is motivated to propel herself forward. It is a baby's visual focus on a toy that stimulates her to elevate her body up off the floor onto her knees and elbows. At six months, babies move in symmetrical-push patterns by tucking toes, flexing ankles, and pushing with their feet. This prepares them for a push-off in belly crawling.

First attempts in belly crawling begin with a lateral weight-shift to one side of the body. One side is elongating as the other side is flexing; one side is supporting, while the other side is ready to move. With one leg flexed and one leg extended, babies ready themselves for belly crawling.

During this month, the baby's increased mobility stimulates alternating knee flexion and knee extension with both legs. From extended elbows babies move down to their forearms for play.

With a push of the left foot into the reach of her left hand, Elle reaches forward to contact the rainbow tower. She taps the tower with her open hand and the tower topples over.

Visual interest in the colored discs on the floor stimulates a lateral weight-shift. This elongates the weight-bearing side of her body with lateral flexion and foot positioning on the opposite side.

Lateral-Push Patterns in Play

Elle supports herself on her left forearm, freeing her right hand to play with a toy.

Although she is weight-bearing on her forearm, this is a more dynamic position. Her left side is supporting while her right side is ready to move—with her toes tucked for push-off she is ready to follow the rolling toy.

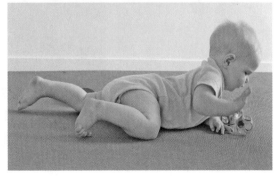

In the next month when babies move in this way on alternate sides, they will crawl forward on their bellies. Differentiating both sides of the body contributes to your baby's developing body image and establishes a broad base for integrating both right-side and left-side functions.

The reach and pull actions are patterns of *elongation* that develop through the baby's relationship to *space*. In these patterns babies practice reaching forward, developing the streamlined mobility and lightness needed to explore their environment.

Tracking a Bouncy Ball Together

Six-month-old babies use the symmetrical forearm position in play interactions. Elle has very good head and neck control and looks up to watch her mother's hand let go of the yellow ball. After the ball drops, even though the ball is close to the floor, Elle's eyes still focus on her mother's hand.

Elle hears the ball bounce on the floor and closes her eyes. Although the sound lets Elle know the ball hit the floor, the ball rebounds quickly, bouncing up again. At six months babies can't adjust their visual focus that quickly. Closing her eyes is a whole body response and she lifts and flexes her forelegs too. The ball bounces lower, which results in a smaller range of motion within Elle's visual field. As she focuses on the ball again, she smiles.

A six-month-old baby can easily play with a toy within reach. Flexing both legs higher, Elle has one hand on the yellow ball. She pushes against it and watches the ball roll away. Looking at the ball she crosses one leg over the other at her ankles.

Six-month-old babies in the prone position have developed full head control: they can extend, flex, laterally flex, and rotate their head.

Side Lying

Rolling to a side-lying position, Elle puts one foot in front of the other for stability. Because lying on the side frees one hand for reaching, it is a more dynamic position for play. Looking downward Elle notices a yellow cup that is close enough for her to reach.

Laterally righting and rotating her head in this position activates the visual, vestibular, proprioceptive, and kinesthetic senses.

The side-lying movements your baby was developing last month are the same ones she masters this month.

Changing Levels

Elle is problem solving and focuses on the yellow ball in front of her. She isn't interested in the yellow *cup* that she can reach, but is motivated to reach the yellow

ball she is interested in. Her visual focus stimulates a change of level, and she moves up onto her hands and knees beginning to get into the quadruped position.

Elle tucks her toes and pushes with both feet together, and then she ends up on her belly again in the more stable prone position.

When babies initiate the movement by pushing through their feet, the movement sequences though their body simultaneously extending their knees and pushing through their hands to extend their elbows. Babies develop muscle tone and strength when they use both hands to push their whole body up against the resistance of gravity. Tucking her toes, pushing through her hands, and extending her elbows, Elle moves her whole body into this dynamic push-up position.

These symmetrical patterns help your baby connect and integrate her upper and lower body, developing her body awareness and body image.

Reaching Her Goal

Motivated to move, Elle pushes with both feet together. By pushing through her toes, she propels her whole body forward to reach and grasp the yellow ball in her hand—reaching her goal.

Tracking a Rolling Ball

The yellow ball rolls to Elle's right side. Supported on her left side, Elle directs her visual attention to reach with her right hand to get the ball. She positions her right foot on the floor for balance and stability.

Rolling balls are unpredictable and judging distance while tracking a rolling ball improves eye-hand-body coordination and spatial awareness.

Exploring a Spiral Rattle

Tomas is holding the spiral rattle with multi-colored wooden beads and two large disk-like beads, one at each end. This is the same rattle that you saw Elle exploring when she was four months old.

He begins grasping this spiral rattle with both hands. Then, the red bead captures his attention.

Following a Red and Orange Bead

Tomas grasps the toy in his right hand and supports himself on his left forearm. He places the rattle on the floor and looks at the red bead.

Problem Solving

Problem solving the task at hand, for a brief moment Tomas pauses. Which hand will he use to grasp the toy and which hand will he use to explore the bead?

Decision Making

Tomas grasps the toy in his left hand. By supporting himself on his left forearm, he frees his right hand for reaching. Now Tomas can use his right hand to explore the orange bead. He holds the toy and by keeping the next yellow bead stationary, Tomas isolates the orange bead and slides it easily on the wire.

Grasp and Fine Motor Skills

Tomas holds the toy rattle with one hand while his other hand manipulates and measures the beads and disk. We have learned in our previous vignettes that babies can isolate their fingers; therefore, now they can use more precise grasping patterns. Tomas grasps and holds the small, orange bead between his thumb and fingertips.

Exploring the large flat bead, Tomas measures its depth with his little finger, and extends his other fingers spreading them across the surface of the broad disk to its edge. He grasps the thin black wire between his thumb and index finger.

  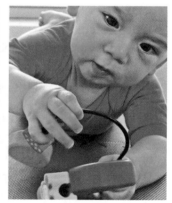

Let's review what Tomas is discovering through his concentrated attention and haptic explorations.

- Color: First Tomas follows the red bead but chooses the orange one.
- Size: He discriminates between the large disk that is fixed to the wire, and the small bead that moves on the wire. The wire is thin and long.
- Shape: Tomas also discriminates between shapes. The red disk is flat, the orange bead is round, and the wire is a spiral shape.

Mastery and Social Sharing

Still holding the toy in his left hand Tomas turns his head and looks up at his mother to share his mastery. A few minutes later Tomas transfers the spiral see-saw toy to his right hand and flexes his right leg. It looks like he is getting ready to push off and start belly crawling.

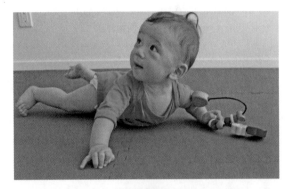

With greater control of his arms and legs, he will soon be able to coordinate his body to navigate new pathways through his environment. This is a period of dynamic discovery of himself—in action and interaction. Your active six-month-old explorer will soon be going where he wants to get what he wants.

Spatial Explorations

Spatial skills are an essential part of everyday life and functioning, for babies and adults. The baby's new movement patterns create opportunities for him to explore his body in new spatial relationships and then move farther afield to explore his environment. Mastery of rolling over, from back to front and front to back, is one of the first ways babies change their place in space. This month a baby may roll over several times in one direction, covering more space on the floor.

Up Off the Floor

In tune with himself, your baby may be exploring novel experiences in push-ups on his hands and feet, and moving up into the quadruped position on his hands and knees—positions that challenge his balance and equilibrium.

Moving Backward before Forward

In tummy-time play, your baby may look perplexed when she ends up pushing herself backward, moving farther away from her goal. Before long, she will be able to move forward in a belly-crawling pattern across the room to reach that enticing toy, plant, or household pet.

Up-and-Over Body Games

Social interactions with your baby have progressed so that you and your baby can now play games together. Before your baby can alternate the lateral pattern for belly crawling, she may be interested in climbing up and over your legs. In ball games, it is the ball that is the focus of the game and having fun in playing this game together.

Spatial Concepts

Babies are developing many important cognitive concepts based on their physical experiences, such as over and under, here and there, upside down and topside up, and in and out.

These thrilling activities provide the groundwork for your baby to be body-confident in her physical abilities, self-confident in her social relationships, and self-motivated in learning.

Six Month Chapter Review

• • • • •

DEVELOPMENTAL MOVEMENT

- Spinal-movement patterns: Babies begin rolling over from the side-lying position onto their back.
- Symmetrical-movement patterns: Babies push with both hands and move backwards in a new locomotion pattern.
- Lateral-movement patterns: Lateral patterns include movement of the arm and leg on the same side of the body together; this is one half of the belly crawling pattern.
- Visual tracking: Babies can follow and begin adjusting their focus to a bouncing ball.
- Changing levels: Babies change levels in push-ups and from the prone position up onto hands and knees.

SOCIAL INTERACTION

- Body games: Babies can climb up onto a parent's extended legs.
- Hand games: Hand games between parent and baby create new play opportunities to enhance a baby's social skills.
- Playing with toys: Both parent and baby focus on the toy in a back-and-forth interaction.
- Sharing mastery in play: Babies look up at a parent or caregiver to share their mastery.

• • • • •

SELF-MOTIVATED LEARNING

- Fine motor skills: Babies can hold an object between their thumb and fingertips.
- Object properties: A baby distinguishes between the properties of a toy rattle by color, size, and shape.
- Decision making: Babies choose between different colored beads on a toy rattle.
- Problem solving: By shifting weight to each side, babies can decide which hand to use to explore a toy.

Moving Forward

• • • • •

This has been a marvelous first six months and exciting beginning to your baby's first year. *Your Self-Motivated Baby*'s integrated parenting approach provides the movement framework supported by documented research for you to enhance your baby's physical, social, and cognitive development.

Through your baby's movement development she is now prepared to explore a more complex environment, expanding her range of experience in action and social interaction. She is expressive and playful with a budding sense of humor. In self-directed play, she orchestrates her action plans, problem solving to reach her goals.

Your baby finds new ways to engage everyone around her. Just as you are learning to read your baby's preverbal communication cues, your baby is tuned in to your nonverbal messages. You and your baby will expand your social repertoire together in a way that nurtures your baby's healthy nervous system. Her expressive communication and inventive social games will engage you in more spontaneous movement play.

Your Self-Motivated Baby

Curious and eager to move, your baby is embarking on a new movement journey, expanding horizons, gaining in independence, and making thrilling discoveries in play.

Based on this essential foundation in movement, your baby will confidently explore his environment and put what he learns into action. These formative experiences contribute to shaping your baby's self-confidence and competence in all his future learning.

Moving forward into the exciting locomotion stage, your baby's new found mobility expands the scope of his explorations, interactions, and goal-directed actions in his environment. The best ways to enhance your baby's development are to provide him with freedom and space to move and uninterrupted time to problem solve in play.

From this dynamic foundation you can move forward confidently, parenting your healthy, happy, motivated baby through the language babies know best—body movement.

Notes

● ● ● ● ●

Introduction

1. National Scientific Council on the Developing Child, "The Timing and Quality of Early Experiences Combine to Shape Brain Architecture," Working Paper #5 (February 2008).
2. Karen E. Adolph and Scott R. Robinson, "Motor Development," in *Handbook of Child Psychology and Developmental Science*, 7th ed., ed. Richard M. Lerner, vol. 2, *Cognitive Processes* (New York: Wiley, 2015), 114–57.
3. M.H. Bornstein, C.S. Hahn, and J. T. D. Suwalsky, "Physically Developed and Exploratory Young Infants Contribute to Their Own Long-Term Academic Achievement." Psychological Science 24, no. 10 (2013).
4. Thomas R. Verny and Pamela Weintraub, *Tomorrow's Baby: The Art and Science of Parenting from Conception through Infancy* (New York: Simon & Schuster, 2002).
5. Stephen Porges, *The Polyvagal Theory: Neurophysiological Foundations of Emotions, Attachment, Communication, and Self-Regulation* (New York: W. W. Norton, 2011).
6. Bornstein, et al. "Physically Developed and Exploratory Young Infants."
7. National Scientific Council on the Developing Child, "Building the Brain's 'Air Traffic Control' System: How Early Experiences Shape the Development of Executive Function," Working Paper #11 (February 2011).
8. Warren Lamb and Eden Davies, *A Framework for Understanding Movement: My Seven Creative Concepts* (London: Brechin Books, 2012).

Month One

1. Porges, *The Polyvagal Theory*.
2. Colwyn Trevarthen, "The Generation of Human Meaning: How Shared Experience Grows in Infancy," in *Joint Attention: New Developments in Psychology, Philosophy of Mind, and Social Neuroscience,* ed. Axel Seemann (Cambridge, MA: MIT Press, 2011).

Month Four

1. Sarah Lloyd et al., "Cortical Activation to Action Perception Is Associated with Action Production Abilities in Young Infants," *Cerebral Cortex*, August 23, 2013.

Month Five

1. Vasudevi Reddy, *How Infants Know Minds* (Cambridge, MA: Harvard /University Press, 2010) doi:10.1093/cercor/bht207.

Bibliography

Adamson, Lauren B., and Connie L. Russell. "Emotion Regulation and the Emergence of Joint Attention." In *Early Social Cognition Understanding Others in the First Months of Life*, edited by Philippe Rochat. New York: Psychology Press, 2014.

Adolph, Karen E., and Kari S. Kretch. "Gibson's Theory of Perceptual Learning." In *International Encyclopedia of Social and Behavioral Sciences*. 2nd ed., edited by James D. Wright. Oxford: Elsevier Science, 2015.

Adolph, Karen E., and Scott R. Robinson. "Motor Development." In *Handbook of Child Psychology and Developmental Science*. 7th ed., edited by Richard M. Lerner, 113–57. Vol. 2. *Cognitive Processes*. New York: Wiley, 2015.

Ambrosini, Ettore, Vasudevi Reddy, Annette De Looper, Marcello Costantini, Beatriz Lopez, and C. Sinigaglia. "Looking Ahead: Anticipatory Gaze and Motor Ability in Infancy." Edited by Markus Lappe. *PLoS ONE* 8, no. 7 (2013): E67916. doi:10.1371/journal.pone.0067916.

Amighi, Janet Kestenberg, Susan Loman, Penny Lewis, and K. Mark Sossin. *The Meaning of Movement: Developmental and Clinical Perspectives of the Kestenberg Movement Profile*. Amsterdam: Gordon and Breach, 1999.

Bahrick, Lorraine E. "Intermodal Perception and Selective Attention to Intersensory Redundancy: Implications for Typical Social Development and Autism." *The Wiley-Blackwell Handbook of Infant Development*, edited by J. Gavin Bremner and Theodore D. Wachs, 120–66. Chichester, UK: Wiley-Blackwell, 2010.

Barker, Jane E., Andrei D. Semenov, Laura Michaelson, Lindsay S. Provan, Hannah R. Snyder, and Yuko Munakata. "Less-Structured Time in Children's Daily Lives Predicts Self-directed Executive Functioning." *Frontiers in Psychology* 5 (2014). doi:10.3389/fpsyg.2014.00593.

Beier, Jonathan S., and Elizabeth S. Spelke. "Infants' Developing Understanding of Social Gaze." *Child Development* 83, no. 2 (2012): 486–96. doi:10.1111/j.1467-8624.2011.01702.x.

Best, John R. "Effects of Physical Activity on Children's Executive Function: Contributions of Experimental Research on Aerobic Exercise." *Developmental Review* 30, no. 4 (2010): 331–51. doi:10.1016/j.dr.2010.08.001.

Bhatt, Ramesh S., and Paul C. Quinn. "How Does Learning Impact Development in Infancy? The Case of Perceptual Organization." *Infancy* 16, no. 1 (2011): 2–38. doi:10.1111/j.1532-7078.2010.00048.x.

Bly, Lois. *Motor Skills Acquisition in the First Year: An Illustrated Guide to Normal Development.* Tucson, AZ: Therapy Skill Builders, 1994.

Bornstein, M. H., C.-S. Hahn, and J. T. D. Suwalsky. "Physically Developed and Exploratory Young Infants Contribute to Their Own Long-Term Academic Achievement." *Psychological Science* 24, no. 10 (2013): 1906–917. doi:10.1177/0956797613479974.

Brown, Stuart L., and Christopher C. Vaughan. *Play: How It Shapes the Brain, Opens the Imagination, and Invigorates the Soul.* New York: Avery, 2010.

Cannon, Erin N., and Amanda L. Woodward. "Infants Generate Goal-Based Action Predictions." *Developmental Science* 15, no. 2 (2012): 292–98. doi:10.1111/j.1467-7687.2011.01127.x.

Carpenter, Malinda, and Kristin Liebal. "Joint Attention, Communication, and Knowing Together in Infancy." In *Joint Attention: New Developments in Psychology, Philosophy of Mind, and Social Neuroscience*, edited by Axel Seemann. Cambridge, MA: MIT Press, 2011.

Case-Smith, J., R. Bigsby, and J. Clutter. "Perceptual-Motor Coupling in the Development of Grasp." *American Journal of Occupational Therapy* 52, no. 2 (1998): 102–10. doi:10.5014/ajot.52.2.102.

Cohen, Bonnie Bainbridge, Lisa Nelson, and Nancy Stark Smith. *Sensing, Feeling, and Action: The Experiential Anatomy of Body-Mind Centering.* Northampton, MA: Contact Editions, 2008.

Corbetta, Daniela, and Esther Thelen. "The Developmental Origins of Bimanual Coordination: A Dynamic Perspective." *Journal of Experimental Psychology: Human Perception and Performance* 22, no. 2 (1996): 502–22. doi:10.1037/0096-1523.22.2.502.

Corbetta, Daniela, Sabrina L. Thurman, Rebecca F. Wiener, Yu Guan, and Joshua L. Williams. "Mapping the Feel of the Arm with the Sight of the Object: On the Embodied Origins of Infant Reaching." *Frontiers in Psychology* 5, no. 576 (2014). doi:10.3389/fpsyg.2014.00576.

Corbetta, Daniela, Yu Guan, and Joshua L. Williams. "Infant Eye-Tracking in the Context of Goal-Directed Actions." *Infancy* 17, no. 1 (2012): 102–25. doi:10.1111/j.1532-7078.2011.00093.x.

Craighero, Laila, Irene Leo, Carlo Umiltà, and Francesca Simion. "Newborns' Preference for Goal-Directed Actions." *Cognition* 120, no. 1 (2011): 26–32. doi:10.1016/j.cognition.2011.02.011.

Elkind, David. *The Power of Play: Learning What Comes Naturally.* Cambridge, MA: Da Capo Lifelong, 2007.

Elsner, Claudia, Marta Bakker, Katharina Rohlfing, and Gustaf Gredeback. "Infants'

Online Perception of Give-and-Take Interactions." *Journal of Experimental Child Psychology* 126 (2014): 280–94.

Fantasia, Valentina, Hanne De Jaegher, and Alessandra Fasulo. "We Can Work It Out: An Enactive Look at Cooperation." *Frontiers in Psychology* 5 (2014). doi:10.3389 /fpsyg.2014.00874.

Ferrari, Pier F., and Giacomo Rizzolatti, eds. *Mirror Neuron Research: The Past and the Future*. London: Philosophical Transactions of the Royal Society B: Biological, 2014. doi:10.1098/rstb.2013.0169.

Filipi, Anna. *Toddler and Parent Interaction: The Organisation of Gaze, Pointing and Vocalisation*. Amsterdam: John Benjamins, 2009.

Frank, Ruella, and Frances La Barre. *The First Year and the Rest of Your Life: Movement, Development, and Psychotherapeutic Change*. New York: Routledge, 2011.

Galinsky, Ellen. *Mind in the Making: The Seven Essential Life Skills Every Child Needs*. New York: HarperStudio, 2010.

Gallagher, Shaun. *How the Body Shapes the Mind*. Oxford: Clarendon Press, 2005.

Gallagher, Shaun. "Interactive Coordination in Joint Attention." In *Joint Attention: New Developments in Psychology, Philosophy of Mind, and Social Neuroscience*, edited by Axel Seemann, 291–305. Cambridge, MA: MIT Press, 2011.

Gerson, Sarah A., and Amanda L. Woodward. "Learning From Their Own Actions: The Unique Effect of Producing Actions on Infants' Action Understanding." *Child Development* 85, no. 1 (February 2014): 264–77. doi:10.1111/cdev.12115.

Goddard, Sally. *The Genius of Natural Childhood: Secrets of Thriving Children*. Stroud, UK: Hawthorn, 2011.

Goldman, Ellen. *As Others See Us: Body Movement and the Art of Successful Communication*. New York: Gordon and Breach, 1994.

Gopnik, Alison. *The Philosophical Baby: What Children's Minds Tell Us about Truth, Love, and the Meaning of Life*. New York: Farrar, Straus and Giroux, 2009.

Hackney, Peggy. *Making Connections Total Body Integration through Bartenieff Fundamentals*. Amsterdam: Gordon and Breach , 1998.

Hofsten, Claes Von. "Action in Development." *Developmental Science* 10, no. 1 (2007): 54–60. doi:10.1111/j.1467-7687.2007.00564.x.

Hofsten, Claes Von. "An Action Perspective on Motor Development." *Trends in Cognitive Sciences* 8, no. 6 (2004): 266–72. doi:10.1016/j.tics.2004.04.002.

Hofsten, Claes Von. "Action, the Foundation for Cognitive Development." *Scandinavian Journal of Psychology* 50, no. 6 (2009): 617–23. doi:10.1111/j.1467-9450.2009.00780.x.

Hofsten, Claes Von., and Kerstin Rosander, eds. *From Action to Cognition*. Amsterdam: Elsevier, 2007.

Iacoboni, Marco. *Mirroring People: The Science of Empathy and How We Connect with Others*. New York: Picador, 2009.

Lamb, Warren, and Eden Davies. *A Framework for Understanding Movement: My Seven Creative Concepts*. London: Brechin Books, 2012.

Lederman, S. J., and R. L. Klatzky. "Haptic Perception: A Tutorial." *Attention, Perception & Psychophysics* 71, no. 7 (2009): 1439–459. doi:10.3758/APP.71.7.1439.

Libertus, Klaus, and Amy Needham. "Encouragement Is Nothing without Control: Factors Influencing the Development of Reaching and Face Preference." *Journal of Motor Learning and Development* 2 (2014): 16–27. doi:10.1123/jmld.2013-0019.

Lloyd-Fox, Sarah, Rachel Wu, John E. Richards, Clare E. Elwell, and Mark H. Johnson. "Cortical Activation to Action Perception Is Associated with Action Production Abilities in Young Infants." *Cerebral Cortex*, August 23, 2013. doi:10.1093/cercor/bht207.

Malloch, Stephen, and Colwyn Trevarthen. *Communicative Musicality: Exploring the Basis of Human Companionship*. Oxford: Oxford University Press, 2009.

Medina, John. *Brain Rules for Baby: How to Raise a Smart and Happy Child from Zero to Five*. Seattle, WA: Pear Press, 2010.

Meltzoff, A. N., and J. Decety. "What Imitation Tells Us about Social Cognition: A Rapprochement between Developmental Psychology and Cognitive Neuroscience." *Philosophical Transactions of the Royal Society B: Biological Sciences* 358, no. 1431 (2003): 491–500. doi:10.1098/rstb.2002.1261.

Meltzoff, Andrew N. "'Like Me': A Foundation for Social Cognition." *Developmental Science* 10, no. 1 (2007): 126–34. doi:10.1111/j.1467-7687.2007.00574.x.

——. "The 'like Me' Framework for Recognizing and Becoming an Intentional Agent." *Acta Psychologica* 124, no. 1 (2007): 26–43. doi:10.1016/j.actpsy.2006.09.005.

Miller, Gill Wright, Pat Ethridge, and Kate Tarlow Morgan. *Exploring Body-Mind Centering: An Anthology of Experience and Method*. Berkeley, CA: North Atlantic Books, 2011.

Moore, Carol-Lynne, and Kaoru Yamamoto. *Beyond Words: Movement Observation and Analysis*. Milton Park, Abingdon, UK: Routledge, 2012.

Moore, Carol-Lynne. *Movement and Making Decisions: The Body-Mind Connection in the Workplace*. New York: Dance & Movement Press, 2005.

Nagy, Emese, Hajnalka Compagne, Hajnalka Orvos, Attila Pal, Peter Molnar, Imre Janszky, Katherine A. Loveland, and Gyorgy Bardos. "Index Finger Movement Imitation by Human Neonates: Motivation, Learning, and Left-Hand Preference." *Pediatric Research* 58, no. 4 (2005): 749–53. doi:10.1203/01.PDR.0000180570.28111.D9.

Nagy, Emese, Karen Pilling, Hajnalka Orvos, and Peter Molnar. "Imitation of Tongue

Protrusion in Human Neonates: Specificity of the Response in a Large Sample."
Developmental Psychology 49, no. 9 (2013): 1628–638. doi:10.1037/a0031127.

National Scientific Council on the Developing Child, "Early Experiences Can Alter Gene Expression and Affect Long-Term Development." Working Paper #10: May 2010. http://developingchild.harvard.edu/index.php/resources/reports_and _working_papers/working_papers/wp10/.

———. "The Timing and Quality of Early Experiences Combine to Shape Brain Architecture." Working Paper #5: February 2008. http://developingchild.harvard.edu /index.php/resources/reports_and_working_papers/working_papers/wp5/.

———. "Building the Brain's 'Air Traffic Control' System: How Early Experiences Shape the Development of Executive Function." Working Paper #11: February 2011. http://developingchild.harvard.edu/resources/reports_and_working_papers /working_papers/wp11/.

Noë, Alva. *Action in Perception*. Cambridge, MA: MIT Press, 2004.

Piek, Jan P. *Infant Motor Development*. Champaign, IL: Human Kinetics, 2006.

Porges, Stephen W. *The Polyvagal Theory: Neurophysiological Foundations of Emotions, Attachment, Communication, and Self-Regulation*. New York: W. W. Norton, 2011.

Potier, Claire, Adrien Meguerditchian, and Jacqueline Fagard. "Handedness for Bimanual Coordinated Actions in Infants as a Function of Grip Morphology." *Laterality: Asymmetries of Body, Brain and Cognition* 18, no. 5 (2013): 576–93. doi:10. 1080/1357650X.2012.732077.

Powers, Niki, and Colwyn Trevarthen. "Voices of Shared Emotion and Meaning: Young Infants and Their Mothers in Scotland and Japan." In *Communicative Musicality: Exploring the Basis of Human Companionship*, edited by Stephen Malloch and Colwyn Trevarthen. Oxford: Oxford University Press, 2010.

Proske, U., and S. C. Gandevia. "The Kinaesthetic Senses." *The Journal of Physiology* 587, no. 17 (2009): 4139–146. doi:10.1113/jphysiol.2009.175372.

Reddy, Vasudevi. "A Gaze at Grips with Me." In *Joint Attention: New Developments in Psychology, Philosophy of Mind, and Social Neuroscience*, edited by Axel Seemann. Cambridge, MA: MIT Press, 2011.

———. *How Infants Know Minds*. Cambridge, MA: Harvard University Press, 2010.

Rizzolatti, Giacomo, and Corrado Sinigaglia. *Mirrors in the Brain: How Our Minds Share Actions and Emotions*. Oxford: Oxford University Press, 2008.

Rochat, Philippe. *Early Social Cognition: Understanding Others in the First Months of Life*. New York, NY: Psychology Press, 2010.

Seemann, Axel. *Joint Attention: New Developments in Psychology, Philosophy of Mind, and Social Neuroscience*. Cambridge, MA: MIT Press, 2011.

Siegel, Daniel J., and Mary Hartzell. *Parenting from the Inside Out: How a Deeper*

Self-Understanding Can Help You Raise Children Who Thrive. 10th Anniversary Revised Edition. New York: Penguin, 2014.

Solomon, Deborah Carlisle. *Baby Knows Best: Raising a Confident and Resourceful Child, the RIE™ Way*. New York: Little Brown, 2013.

Soska, Kasey C., and Karen E. Adolph. "Postural Position Constrains Multimodal Object Exploration in Infants." *Infancy* 19, no. 2 (2014): 138–61. doi:10.1111/infa.12039.

Soska, Kasey C., Karen E. Adolph, and Scott P. Johnson. "Systems in Development: Motor Skill Acquisition Facilitates Three-Dimensional Object Completion." *Developmental Psychology* 46, no. 1 (2010): 129–38. doi:10.1037/a0014618.

Stern, Daniel N. *Forms of Vitality: Exploring Dynamic Experience in Psychology, the Arts, Psychotherapy, and Development*. Oxford: Oxford University Press, 2010.

——. "Vitality Contours: The Temporal Contour of Feelings as a Basic Unit for Constructing the Infant's Social Experience." In *Early Social Cognition: Understanding Others in the First Months of Life*, edited by Philippe Rochat, 67–80. New York, NY: Psychology Press, 2010.

Stokes, Beverly. *Amazing Babies Moving: Essential Movement to Enhance Your Baby's Development in the First Year*. 2nd ed. Toronto: Move Alive Media, 2009.

Thomas, Brittany L., Jenni M. Karl, and Ian Q. Whishaw. "Independent Development of the Reach and the Grasp in Spontaneous Self-Touching by Human Infants in the First 6 Months." *Frontiers in Psychology* 5, no. 1526 (2014). doi:10.3389/fpsyg.2014.01526.

Tomasello, Michael, and Malinda Carpenter. "Shared Intentionality." *Developmental Science* 10, no. 1 (2007): 121–25. doi:10.1111/j.1467-7687.2007.00573.x.

Tortora, Suzi. *The Dancing Dialogue: Using the Communicative Power of Movement with Young Children*. Baltimore, MD: Paul H. Brookes, 2006.

Trevarthen, Colwyn. "The Generation of Human Meaning: How Shared Experience Grows in Infancy." In *Joint Attention: New Developments in Psychology, Philosophy of Mind, and Social Neuroscience*, edited by Axel Seemann. Cambridge, MA: MIT Press, 2011.

Verny, Thomas R., and John Kelly. *The Secret Life of the Unborn Child*. New York: Summit Books, 1981.

Verny, Thomas R., and Pamela Weintraub. *Tomorrow's Baby: The Art and Science of Parenting from Conception through Infancy*. New York: Simon & Schuster, 2002.

Verny, Thomas R., and Pamela Weintraub. *Pre-Parenting: Nurturing Your Child from Conception*. New York: Simon & Schuster, 2003.

Woodward, Amanda, and Sarah Gerson. "Mirroring and the Development of Action Understanding." *Philosophical Transactions of the Royal Society B: Biological Sciences* 369, no. 1644 (June 5, 2014). doi:10.1098/rstb.2013.0181.

Woodward, Amanda. "Infant Foundations of Intentional Understanding." In *Navigating the Social World: What Infants, Children, and Other Species Can Teach Us*, edited by Mahzarin R. Banaji and Susan A. Gelman. Oxford: Oxford University Press, 2013.

———. "Infants' Grasp of Others' Intentions." *Current Directions in Psychological Science* 18, no. 1 (2009): 53–57. doi:10.1111/j.1467-8721.2009.01605.x.

Yu, Chen, and Linda B. Smith. "Joint Attention without Gaze Following: Human Infants and Their Parents Coordinate Visual Attention to Objects through Eye-Hand Coordination." Edited by Andrew Bremner. *PLoS ONE* 8, no. 11 (2013): E79659. doi:10.1371/journal.pone.0079659.

Index

• • • • •

movement and, 31
of vowels, 9, 29–30

W

Walkers, 68
Walking rhythms, 14–15
Weight-shift patterns, 103,
121, 134, 140–41

Y

"You-ness," authentic, 7, 31

Acknowledgments

● ● ● ● ●

First and foremost I would like to thank all the parents and their babies who participated in my baby movement sessions over many years, and the new group of parents and babies currently involved in my baby and toddler movement research. Their feedback and dialogue have provided an invaluable parent perspective for this book and my training programs.

I would like to thank Dr. Thomas R. Verny, a good friend, the founding president of the Association for Prenatal and Perinatal Psychology and Health (APPPAH), for his enthusiastic support. I am happy and honored that he has written a vivid, inspiring foreword for this book.

During the writing of this book, it has been a great pleasure to participate in many lively and constructive discussions of my ideas with friends and colleagues. I would like to thank Eleanor Criswell Hanna, Ed.D., founder/director of the Novato Institute for Somatic Research and Training and editor of *Somatics Journal*, for her valued comments and stimulating ideas over many meetings; Janet Kaylo, founder/director of the Laban/Bartenieff and Somatic Studies International (LSSI), a friend, colleague, and collaborator in each other's training programs, for our ongoing somatic dialogues that expand each other's perspective; Janet Kwantes, Certified Movement Analyst, for her ongoing support of my work and programs; Susan Bradford, childbirth educator, for our dialogues on workshop ideas to support parents and their babies; Deborah Bowes, DPT, Feldenkrais teacher, and Cliff Smyth, MS, Feldenkrais practitioner, who collaborated on organizing the professional workshop in San Francisco that first introduced the baby movement research in this book.

My work has evolved from in-depth training and collaborative dialogues with noted movement and somatic professionals. Warren Lamb's Movement Pattern Analysis (MPA) approach to how individuals are motivated to make decisions and take action inspired me to document the baby's decision-making process in social interactions and goal-directed actions for this book; Bonnie Bainbridge Cohen, founder of the School for Body-Mind Centering®, whose experiential, somatic, and academic work in infant developmental movement and the body systems inspired many concepts that elucidate my work; Carl Stough, founder of the Stough Institute, who enriched my understanding of each person's unique breathing coordination; Marion Woodman, Jungian analyst and noted author, for our workshops on the interplay between movement, perception, and consciousness we led together for over twelve years.

A special thank you to my partner, Louis Stokes, PhD, psychologist, leadership consultant, executive coach, and author. His professional expertise led to ongoing lively discussions of the baby's developing social and cognitive development that provided new insights and perspectives; his contributions have been vital in creating this inspiring book. And thanks to family members and close friends whose interest and feedback along the way helped make this book more accessible and engaging for parents. Thank you to the parents who provided selected photos of their baby in this book.

With deep appreciation to my publisher Tim McKee at North Atlantic Books for his keen interest in my research approach to infant movement, communication, and learning development that led to the publication of this book. It has been a pleasure to work closely with Hisae Matsuda, who shaped the manuscript into this appealing book; Nancy O'Connor for her clarity in text organization; and book designer Jasmine Hromjak, for her subtle design elements and skillful photo placement.

And thank you to the entire North Atlantic Books team for their collaborative approach in making this book a valuable resource for parents, professionals, and educators.

About the Author

• • • • •

Author, developmental movement researcher, and educator Beverly Stokes is the founder/director of *Amazing Babies Moving®* Training Programs. She is a Certified Movement Analyst (CMA), Movement Pattern Analysis Consultant (MPA), and Registered International Somatic Movement Educator (ISMETA).

Stokes's best-selling parenting book, *Amazing Babies Moving: Essential Movement to Enhance Your Baby's Development in the First Year,* is available in five languages. She has become known for her baby movement research and analysis, which is documented in the longitudinal video movement series, *Amazing Babies Moving* and *Amazing Toddlers Moving.*

Stokes has the unique ability to convey complex baby movement research concepts in useful and visually appealing photo-vignettes that inspire and educate parents, educators, and professionals. In her recent work Beverly expands upon the developmental movement foundation that is essential for a social, competent, and motivated baby.

With over twenty-five years experience working with babies, children, and adults, Stokes is acknowledged as a leader in the field of developmental movement education and nonverbal communication. Her internationally recognized published work has been integrated into curricula in university graduate and undergraduate programs in early childhood education, occupational and physical therapy, optometry, and psychology. Her work has also been applied in Montessori infancy and Waldorf daycare programs, and pre-school and parenting programs.

Stokes conducts training programs and workshops for professionals, educators, and parents in the United States and Canada. She also consults and gives talks to educational and professional organizations, preschools, and parenting groups.

For more information on Beverly Stokes's work, please visit www.amazing babiesmoving.com.